1 MONTH OF
FREE
READING

at

www.ForgottenBooks.com

By purchasing this book you are eligible for one month membership to ForgottenBooks.com, giving you unlimited access to our entire collection of over 1,000,000 titles via our web site and mobile apps.

To claim your free month visit:
www.forgottenbooks.com/free1246283

ISBN 978-0-332-76587-7
PIBN 11246283

This book is a reproduction of an important historical work. Forgotten Books uses
state-of-the-art technology to digitally reconstruct the work, preserving the original format
whilst repairing imperfections present in the aged copy. In rare cases, an imperfection in
the original, such as a blemish or missing page, may be replicated in our edition. We do,
however, repair the vast majority of imperfections successfully; any imperfections that
remain are intentionally left to preserve the state of such historical works.

BEAUMARCHAIS

AND HIS TIMES.

SKETCHES OF FRENCH SOCIETY

IN THE EIGHTEENTH CENTURY

FROM UNPUBLISHED DOCUMENTS.

BY

LOUIS DE LOMÉNIE.

TRANSLATED BY HENRY S. EDWARDS.

IN FOUR VOLUMES.
VOL. II.

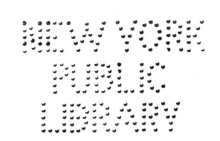

LONDON:
ADDEY AND CO.; HENRIETTA STREET,
COVENT GARDEN.
MDCCCLVI.

LONDON:
WILLIAM STEVENS, PRINTER, 37, BELL YARD,
TEMPLE BAR.

CONTENTS.

———

CHAPTER IX.

CHAPTER X.

CHAPTER XI.

CHAPTER XVI.

CHAPTER XVII.

BEAUMARCHAIS AND HIS TIMES.

CHAPTER IX.

MADAME MENARD.—A PORTRAIT BY GRIMM.—A JEA-
LOUS DUKE.—A REMONSTRANCE FROM BEAUMAR-
CHAIS.—THE RIVALS.—THE DUKE ATTACKS GUDIN.
—THE DUKE ATTACKS BEAUMARCHAIS.

THE details of the incident which is now coming
under our notice are completely unknown to the
public. In his notice of Beaumarchais, La Harpe contents himself with saying that he had a quarrel with a
nobleman who wished to take a courtesan away from
him. The name is rather a hard one for Mademoiselle
Ménard, with whom we are about to make acquaintance, and who was not *precisely* what La Harpe calls
her. In his edition of the works of Beaumarchais,
which has been made the model of all the others,
Gudin, reserving the narrative of his friend's quarrel
with the Duke de Chaulnes, for his Memoirs which
remained unpublished, only printed the two most
vague and insignificant of all the letters relating to
the affair in question.

In the meanwhile the Author of "The Barber of Seville," had carefully collected all the papers relating to this strange affair. The packet which contains them is quite complete: it is one of those on which he has written, with his own hand "Materials for the Memoirs of my own Life;" and as the adventure had occasioned the commencement of judicial proceedings before M. de Sartines, then Lieutenant-General of Police, Beaumarchais, who afterwards became rather intimately acquainted with him, induced him to give back all the letters and depositions of each of the actors who had appeared in this tragi-comic scene. I shall endeavour, then, to reproduce it as it actually occurred, leaving the characters as much as possible to speak in their own words. These pictures of manners, when they are minute and authentic, throw much more light on the character of a period than the most pompous generalities. Let us, first of all, say a word about the amiable person who was the cause of so many combats between Beaumarchais, skilful and prudent as Ulysses, and a duke and peer of France, strong and impetuous as Ajax. Mademoiselle Ménard was a young and pretty, if not virtuous *artiste*, who in June 1770 had appeared with much success at the Italian Theatre, in Madame Laruette's parts; she had above all distinguished herself in that of Louise in "The Deserter." Grimm has given us her portrait. "It is agreed generally enough," he says, in his "Literary Correspondence," " that she played the part of Louise better than any of our most favourite actresses, and that she introduced *nuances* into the character, which were missed by Madame Laruette and Madame Trial. She had less success in the other parts; and it may be said that she played with an unevenness which was really surprising. She has gained many supporters; authors, poets, and musicians are in her interest; in spite of which M. le Maréchal de Richelieu, *kislar-aga* of the amusements of the public, that is to say of plays,* does not wish her to be engaged even on trial. He knows better than we do what we like to have for our money. Mademoiselle Ménard's voice is of mediocre quality, and she has had a bad singing master. With a better system, and the power of regulating her voice, she may be able to sing sufficiently well not to injure the effect of her acting. As regards the latter, she has first of all the advantages of an easy delivery and a natural pronunciation. She does not speak from the head, and in *alto* tones, like Madame Laruette and Madame Trial. Her face is that of a handsome girl, but not of a pleasing actress. Put Mademoiselle Ménard, with her freshness, youth, and piquancy, down to supper by the side of Mademoiselle Arnould, and the latter will appear a skeleton in comparison; but

* In his capacity of first gentleman of the King's Chamber.

on the stage this skeleton will be graceful, distinguished, and charming, while the fresh and
piquante Ménard will look like a slut (*gaupe*).* Her
head appears to be rather large; and her cheek bones
are rather too high, which impedes the play of the
countenance. A great deal has been said about the
beauty of her arms; they are very white, but too
short; they look like lions' paws; her face generally
is rather too large, and strongly marked† for the naïve,
ingenuous, gentle heroines such as the majority of
those of our *opéras comiques*.‡ . . . . . For the rest,
I am of the opinion of the public that Mademoiselle
Ménard ought to be received on trial; she appears
capable of being made very useful. It is said that
she was in the first instance a flower girl on the
boulevards; but that, wishing to abandon this calling,
which has rather degenerated from its original im-

---

* I must apologise to readers who are delicate in the choice of
their expressions, for quoting some of Grimm's words literally. They
have, however, an historic importance; above all, when we remember
that Grimm's articles formed the delight of a sufficiently large number of German princes and princesses, who paid considerable prices for
them.

† This portrait of Grimm's will be rather modified directly by a
worthy abbé, who tells us that gentleness was the distinct characteristic of Mademoiselle Ménard's physiognomy.

‡ An *opéra comique* is any opera in which spoken dialogue
occurs, and cannot therefore be rendered by "comic opera." The
French version of the "Sonnambula," for instance, in which most of
the recitative is omitted, is entitled "Opéra Comique."—TRANS.

portance, at the period when Glycera sold bouquets at the gates of the Athenian Temples, she purchased Restaut's Grammar, and applied herself to the study of the French language and pronunciation, after which she tried her powers of acting. One thing is certain, that during her *débuts*, she applied to all the authors, whether composers or poets, in order to obtain their advice and profit by their intelligence, and this with a zeal and docility which have been rewarded by the applause she has received in her different parts. M. de Péquigny, now Duke de Chaulnes, the protector of her charms, has had her portrait painted by Greuze; so that if we do not keep her on the stage, we shall at all events see her at the next exhibition.*

The protection of the Duke de Chaulnes having doubtless prevented Mademoiselle Ménard from being protected by the Duke de Richelieu, she sacrificed her hopes of success to the jealousy of the first of these two dukes, and renounced the stage; but as she was witty and agreeable, she received very distinguished guests (of the male sex, it must be understood), Marmontel, Sedaine, Rulhiéres Chamfort, together with the highest nobles, who were brought there by the Duke de Chaulnes. This duke, who was then thirty, was already notorious for the violence and eccentricity of his disposition. He was the

* Correspondance Littéraire.

last representative of the younger branch of the house of Luynes, which I think became extinct in his person. Gudin's unpublished manuscript contains some details about him, which are corroborated by all contemporaneous evidence. "His disposition," writes Gudin, "was a strange mixture of good qualities and defects of the most opposite nature. Wit without judgment; pride, and yet such a deficiency in discernment as to deprive him of the consciousness of his own dignity in his relations with his superiors, his equals, or his inferiors; a vast but ill-regulated memory; a great desire to acquire knowledge, and a still greater taste for dissipation; prodigious physical strength; a violence of temper which interfered with his reason, in itself always sufficiently confused; liability to fits of passion, in which he resembled a drunken savage, not to say a wild beast; always giving himself up to the impression of the moment, without reference to the consequences, he had got himself into more than one dilemma; banished from the kingdom for five years, he had employed the period of his exile in a scientific journey; he had visited the pyramids, associated with the Bedouins of the desert, brought back many objects of natural history and an unhappy monkey, which he overwhelmed with blows every day.* The Duke de

* We may add to this portrait of Gudin, that the Duke de Chaulnes, in the midst of his disorderly and extravagant life, had

Chaulnes' temper rendered his *liaison* with Mademoiselle Ménard a very quarrelsome one; jealous, unfaithful, and violent, he had for some time inspired her with no other feeling than that of fear, when he suddenly took a great fancy to Beaumarchais, and introduced him to his mistress. At the end of some months, he perceived that she preferred Beaumarchais to him: his love changed to anger; Mademoiselle Ménard, frightened by his violence, begged Beaumarchais to discontinue his visits. Out of regard to her, he consented to do so; but as the duke still continued his ill treatment, she became desperate, and took refuge in a convent. When she considered she had regained her liberty by a final rupture, she returned to her house, inviting Beaumarchais to come and see her.

At this moment Beaumarchais wrote to the Duke de Chaulnes, and proposed to him a somewhat singular treaty of peace, in a letter which is somewhat curious,

preserved some of his father's tastes, who was a distinguished *savant* in mechanics, physics, and natural history, and who died an honorary member of the Academy of Sciences. The son was passionately fond ot chemistry, and made some discoveries in relation to it. Still, even in this kind of occupation he was remarkable for the eccentricity of his disposition. Thus, in order to test the efficacy of a preparation he had invented against asphyxia, he shut himself up in a glass closet calculated to induce asphyxia, leaving to his valet the task of coming to his succour from time to time, and trying the effect of his remedy upon him. Luckily he had an attentive servant, who did not let him go too far.

both from its substance and from its style, which is
a mixture of familiarity, freedom, prudence, and
respect, representing well enough the difference in
the temper and social position of the two persons.
Here is the letter. It must not be forgotten that
Beaumarchais was at first very intimate with the
Duke de Chaulnes.

"M. le Duc,—Madame Ménard * informs me that she has
returned to her house, and invites me to go and see her, like
all her other friends, whenever I please. I have come to the
opinion that the reasons which forced her to go away have
ceased to exist; she informs me that she is free, and I congratulate you both sincerely upon it. I intend to see her to-morrow,
during the day. Force of circumstances has, then, had that
effect on your determination, which my representations had
been unable to produce. You have ceased to torment her.
I am delighted for the sake of both—I might say for that of all
three. If I had not, then, resolved to put myself entirely out
of the question in all affairs in which the interests of this unfortunate creature are engaged, I know by what pecuniary
sacrifices you have endeavoured to replace her under your protection, and in how noble a manner she has crowned her disinterested conduct of six years, by bringing back to M. de Genlis
the money you had borrowed from him to offer her. What kind
heart is there that would not be warmed by such conduct? As
for me, whose offers to serve her she has hitherto refused, I
shall consider myself much honoured, if not in the eyes of the
whole world, at all events in my own, by her consenting to
number me amongst the number of her most devoted friends.
Ah! M. le Duc, the affection of so generous a heart can be retained neither by threats, nor by blows, nor by money.

* It will be seen that all the friends of this young lady called her
Madame, to which, however, no importance must be attached.

Excuse me if I indulge in these reflections : they are not without reference to the object I have in view in writing to you. When I speak to you of Madame Ménard, I forget my personal interest ; I forget that after having done all I could to serve you, receiving all sorts of attentions from you, both at your house and at mine, and making sacrifices which my attachment to you could alone have induced ; * that after pitying me, and telling me very disparaging things about her, you suddenly, without any cause, changed both in your conversation and conduct, and said a hundred worse things to her about me, than you had said to me about her. I pass in silence over the scene, which was horrible for her, and disgusting between two men, in which you so far forget yourself as to taunt me with being the son of a watchmaker. As I am proud of my parents, even before those who think themselves entitled to insult their own,† you must perceive, M. le Duc, what an advantage I had over you at this moment, from our respective positions ; and without the unjustifiable anger which has misled you ever since, you would certainly have felt obliged to me for the moderation with which I repelled the insult of one whom I had always professed to honour and love with my whole heart. If my respectful regard for you was not able to lead me so far as to fear a man, it is because that is not in my power. Is this a reason for entertaining any bad feeling towards me? and ought not my moderation of every description to have, on the contrary, all the value in your eyes which it derives from the fact of my not being deficient in firmness. I thought you would recover from such a multitude of unjust feelings, and that my considerate conduct would at length make you ashamed of your own. Whatever you have done, you have no more suc-

---

* He had lent the duke money.

† Alluding to a law-suit the Duke de Chaulnes had at that time with his mother, of whom he spoke very ill.

ceeded in forming a bad opinion of me yourself, than in giving
one to Madame Ménard. She required, for her own interest,
that I should not see her; and as it is not dishonourable to
obey a woman, I was two entire months without visiting her,
or having any communication with her. She now allows me to
augment the number of her friends. If, during this time, you
have not regained the advantages which your negligence and
your irritability caused you to lose, it must be that the means
you employed were not the proper ones.   Now, believe
me, M. le Duc; give up an error which has been the cause of
so much grief to you.   I never sought to diminish the tender
affection which this generous woman had devoted to you;
she would have despised me if I had attempted it. You have
had no enemy to interfere with her but yourself.   The injury
your last acts of violence have done you, points out the road
you must follow, if you wish to find yourself again at the
head of her real friends. . . . . Instead of the infernal
life you make her lead, let us all unite to procure a calm and
agreeable existence for her.   Remember all I have had the
honour to say to you on this subject; and, for her sake, restore your friendship to one whom you have been unable to
deprive of the esteem he has for you. If this letter does not
open your eyes, I shall think I have fulfilled all my duties
towards my friend, to whom I have offered no offence, whose
insults I have forgotten, and to whom I now appeal for the
last time, assuring him that if this step be productive of no
effects, I shall confine myself to the cold, distant, severe
respect which should be entertained for a man of rank,
about whose disposition one has been grossly deceived."

The Duke de Chaulnes did not answer this letter;
some months passed, during which Beaumarchais,
although the duke did not authorise his visits, appears to have profited by the permission given him

by Mademoiselle Ménard to recommence calling upon her. At last, one fine morning, February 11, 1773, the Duke de Chaulnes took it into his head to kill his rival. As the following scene lasted an entire day, and as each of the actors who took part in it made his deposition in writing before the Lieutenant of Police, or the Tribunal of the Marshals of France, as regarded his own share in the transaction, I will compare the different depositions, commencing with that of Gudin, who saw the commencement of the storm. In the unpublished narrative which he prepared of the whole affair thirty-five years after the event, Gudin colours a little. I prefer his deposition, as made at the time: he appears more natural in it. We see that he is young, good-natured, devoted to Beaumarchais, with whom he had been acquainted some time, and who had, doubtless, introduced him to Mademoiselle Ménard, but very susceptible, not very warlike, and much afraid of compromising himself.

Report made to the Lieutenant of Police, of what happened to me on Thursday, February 11.

"On Thursday, at eleven in the morning, I went to Madame Ménard's, after having been to several places. 'It is a long while since I have seen you,' she said; 'I thought you no longer cared for me.' I assured her of the contrary, and took a seat in an arm-chair, by the side of her bed. She burst into tears, and, unable to contain her grief, told me how much she had had to suffer from the violence of the Duke de Chaulnes. She afterwards spoke to me of an accusation made against M. de Beaumarchais. The Duke entered; I rose, bowed to him, and gave him my place by the side of the bed. 'I am crying,' said Madame Ménard, 'and begging M. Gudin to induce M. de Beaumarchais to justify himself from the ridiculous accusation made against him.' 'What necessity is there,' replied the duke, 'for justifying a scoundrel like Beaumarchais?' 'He is a very honest man,' she replied, shedding fresh tears. 'You love him,' cried the duke, rising. 'You humiliate me; and I declare I will go out and fight with him. There was, in the room where we were, a friend of Madame Ménard's, a servant, or lady's maid, and a young child, the daughter of Madame Ménard. We all got up with shrieks. Madame Ménard jumped out of bed; I ran after the duke, who went out, in spite of my resistance, and locked the door of the ante-chamber upon me. I went back to the apartment and cried out to the alarmed women, 'I am going to Beaumarchais, I will prevent this. duel.' I started from the neighbourhood of the Italian Theatre, where she lives, in the direction of the Hôtel de Condé, opposite where M. de Beaumarchais lives. I met his carriage in the Rue Dauphine, near the Carrefour de Bussy. I threw myself on the horses' heads, and then spoke to him at the window. 'The duke is looking out for you, to fight with you. Come to my house; I will tell you the rest.' 'I am going to the Captainry to hold a sitting; I will go to your house when it is finished.'* He went off. I followed the carriage with my eyes, and then took the road to my own house; as I was ascending the steps of the Pont Neuf, from the Quay de Conti, I felt myself stopped by the

---

* Here Gudin weakens both his own remark and Beaumarchais' answer, for fear of injuring him. His real words, as restored in his manuscript, and in Beaumarchais' deposition, were these:—"The Duke is looking for you to kill you." Beaumarchais' answer was, "He will only kill his own fleas."

skirt of my coat, and fell back into the arms of the Duke
de Chaulnes, who, being much taller and stronger than myself, carried me off like a bird of prey, threw me, in spite of
my resistance, into a hackney-coach, from which he had got
down, cried out ' Rue de Condé' to the coachman, and told
me, with an oath, that I should find Beaumarchais for him.
' By what right,' I said, ' M. le Duc, do you, who are always
talking about liberty, dare to attack mine ?' ' By the right
of the stronger ; you'll find Beaumarchais for me, or . . .
' M. le Duc, I have no arms, and you will not assassinate me,
probably.' ' No, I shall only kill this Beaumarchais, and when
I have plunged my sword into his body, and have torn his
heart out with my teeth, this Ménard will become what she
may.' (I suppress the execrable oaths by which these words
were accompanied.) ' I do not know where M. de Beaumarchais
is ; and if I did know, I should not tell you, in the passion in
which you now are.' ' If you resist, I will strike you.' ' I shall
strike you back, M. le Duc.' ' A blow to me ! ' and he at
once threw himself upon me, and endeavoured to take me by
the hair ; but, as I wear a wig, it came off in his hand, which
rendered this scene comic, as I understood from the shouts of
laughter uttered by the populace around the coach, of which
both the windows were open. The duke, who could see nothing, took me by the throat and inflicted several scratches
on my neck, my ear, and my chin. I stopped his blows as
best I could, and called loudly for the guard. He became
more moderate then. I put my wig on again, and declared
to him, that on leaving M. de Beaumarchais, where he was taking me by force, I would follow him nowhere, except before a
commissary. I made all the remonstrances which the confused
state I was in, and the little time I had, would allow. Quite
sure that he would not find M. de Beaumarchais at home,
and equally sure that if they saw me, his servants would not
fail to tell me where their master was, I was in hopes that if
they saw the duke alone, his agitated state would prevent

their telling him. Accordingly, the very moment the duke
jumped out of the carriage, to knock at M. de Beaumarchais'
door, I jumped out also, and returned to my own house, but
by out-of-the way streets, lest the duke should run after me
again."

I suppress that part of Gudin's deposition which
contains what afterwards appears in the other depositions, and only reproduce the termination, on account
of its tone.

" ' There, Sir,' he says, ' is the exact truth of all I saw, and
all that happened to me. I regret it still more, from the
fact that this affair will probably make the Duke de Chaulnes
my irreconcileable enemy, although all I did was to render a
service to himself, in preventing the conflict, which, however,
it might have terminated, could not have failed to have been
fatal to him, above all, under the unfortunate circumstances
by which he is at present surrounded.' I said this to him himself, in the coach where he was keeping me. I am, with the
most profound respect,
    " Sir, &c.,
            " GUDIN DE LA BRENELLERIE."

Let us leave Gudin, running away, but do not let
us quit the Duke de Chaulnes, who was knocking at
Beaumarchais' door.

The servants told him imprudently that their master was at the Louvre at the Tribunal of the Captainry, and he accordingly hurried there, still anxious
to kill him. Beaumarchais, who had been already

warned by Gudin, was passing sentence on offenders against the game laws when he saw his enraged enemy enter. We will now let him speak for himself. What follows is extracted from an unpublished Memorial, which he addressed to the Lieutenant of Police and the Tribunal of the Marshals of France.

Exact Narrative of what took place, Thursday, February 11, 1773, between M. le Duc de Chaulnes and myself, Beaumarchais.

"I had just opened the sittings at the Captainry when I saw M. le Duc de Chaulnes enter with the wildest air imaginable. He told me aloud that he had something important to communicate to me, that I must come out immediately. 'I cannot,' M. le Duc, I replied, 'the public service requires that I should terminate, in a becoming manner, the task I have commenced.' I wished him to sit down; he refused; people were getting astonished at his appearance and manner. I began to fear that the affair would be understood, and suspended the sittings for a moment to go with him into a private room. There he told me, in the energetic language of the public markets, that he wished to kill me on the spot, to tear my heart out, and drink my blood, for which he thirsted. 'Oh! is that all, M. le Duc,' I replied; 'you must allow business to go before pleasure.' I wished to return; he stopped me, telling me he would tear my eyes out before every one if I did not go out with him. 'You would be lost, M. le Duc, if you were mad enough to attempt it. I entered calmly and directed that a seat should be given to him. Surrounded as I was by the officers and guards of the Captainry, I exhibited for two hours, while the sittings lasted, the greatest coolness in opposition to the irritable, wild manner, in which he walked about, disturbing the sittings, and

saying to every one ' Will it be much longer?' * He took M. le
Comte de Marcouville, the officer who was with me, on one side,
and told him that he was waiting to fight with me. M. de Marcouville sat down with a sombre expression. I made a sign to
him to be silent, and continued. M. de Marcouville told M. de
Vintrais, Officer of the Maréchaussée and Inspector of the Preserves. I perceived it, and again made signs for him to remain
silent. I said, ' M. de Chaulnes is lost if it is supposed that he
comes to take me away from here and cut my throat.' When
the sittings were over, I put on my walking-dress, and, going
down to M. de Chaulnes, asked him what he wanted of me,
and what cause of complaint he could have against a man whom
he had not seen for six months. ' No explanation,' he said
to me ; ' let us go and fight directly, or I make a disturbance
here.' ' At least,' I said, ' you will allow me to go to my house
for a sword ? I have only an indifferent mourning sword in my
carriage, with which you do not probably require that I should
defend myself against you.' ' We will call,' he replied, ' at
M. le Comte de Turpin's, who will lend you one, and whom
I wish to be our witness.' He jumped into my carriage
before me ; I got in after him. His carriage followed us.
He did me the honour to assure me that this time I should
not escape, adorning his remarks with all the superb impre-
cations that are so familiar to him. The calmness of my
replies amazed him, and increased his rage. He threatened
me with his fist in the carriage. I observed to him, that if
he intended to fight me, a public insult could only retard his
object, and that I was not going to get my sword, if in the

---

* It is impossible not to notice the comic side of this scene, in
which Beaumarchais, in his judge's robes, probably made the audience
last as long as he could, while the duke, in his anxiety to kill him,
was asking whether "it would be much longer ?" Beaumarchais,
although certainly not wanting in courage, was, doubtless, less in a
hurry than the duke, for the latter was a colossus, and he was
furious, as will be seen, even to madness.

meanwhile I was to fight like a scavenger. We arrived at
M. le Comte de Turpin's, who was going out. He came up
to the carriage. 'M. le Duc,' I said, ' has taken me off without my knowing why; he wishes to cut throats with me;
but in this strange affair he leaves me at least to hope that
you will be willing, Sir, to witness the conduct of the two
adversaries.' M. de Turpin told me that pressing business
forced him to go instantly to the Luxembourg, and that it
would keep him there until four in the afternoon. I had no
doubt that the Count de Turpin's object was to allow a few
hours for a violent temper to get calm. He went away.
M. de Chaulnes wished to keep me in his house until four
o'clock. As for 'that, no, M. le Duc; in the same way that
I would not meet you alone on the ground, on account of
the risk I should run of your accusing me of assassination, if you forced me to wound you, I will not go into a
house of which you are the master, and where you would
not fail to play me a bad turn.' I ordered my coachman
to take me home. 'If you stop there,' said M. de Chaulnes,
' I will stab you at the door.' ' Then you will have that
pleasure,' I said, ' for I shall wait nowhere else, until the
hour which is to show me what your intentions really are.'
His insults were continued while we were in the carriage.
' Stop, M. le Duc,' I said, ' when a man means to fight,
he does not talk so much. Come in, take dinner, and if
I do not succeed in restoring you to your senses between
now and four o'clock, and you persist in forcing me to
the alternative of fighting, or incurring contempt, the fate
of arms will necessarily have to decide the matter.' The
carriage arrived at my door. I got out, he followed, and
pretended to accept my invitation to dinner. I gave my
orders calmly. The footman gave me a letter, when he
rushed towards it and tore it from me, before my father
and all my servants; I wished to turn the affair off as a
joke. He commenced swearing; my father was frightened;

I re-assured him and ordered dinner to be brought to us in
my private room. We went up stairs; my servant followed
me; I asked him for my sword; it was at the furbisher's.
'Go and get it,' I said; 'and if it is not ready bring me another.' 'I forbid you to leave the room,' said M. de Chaulnes,
'or I knock you down.' 'You have changed your intention,
then,' I said. 'Heaven be praised! for I could not fight
without a sword.' I made a sign to my valet, who went out.
I was going to write; he snatched the pen from me. I represented to him that my house was a sanctuary, which I should
not violate unless he forced me to do so, by his outrages. I
wished to commence a parley with him about his insane idea
in wanting positively to kill me. He threw himself upon my
mourning sword, which had been placed on my bureau, and
said to me, with all the rage of a madman, and gnashing his
teeth, that I should go no further. He drew my sword, though
his own was by his side, and was about to rush upon me.
'Coward!' I cried; and, taking him round the body, so as to
get beyond reach of the weapon, I endeavoured to push him
towards the mantelpiece. With the hand he had at liberty he
dug his five claws into my eyes and lacerated my face, which
became bathed in blood. Without loosing my hold I managed
to ring; my servants ran in. 'Disarm this maniac,' I cried,
'while I hold him.' My cook, as brutal and strong as the
duke, took up a log to knock him down. I cried still more
loudly, 'Disarm him, but do not injure him; he would say
I·had attempted to assassinate him in my house.' My sword
was torn away from him. Instantly he sprang at my hair,
and completely stripped my forehead. The pain I experienced made me quit his body, which I was encircling, and
with the full force of my arm I sent a heavy blow with my
fist, straight into his face. 'Wretch!' he exclaimed, 'you
strike a duke, and peer!' I confess that this exclama-
tion, extravagantly absurd at such a moment, would have
made me laugh at any other time; but, as he is stronger

than I am, and had taken me by the throat, I could think
only of defending myself. My coat, my shirt, were torn,
my face was bleeding afresh. My father, an old man of
seventy-five, wished to throw himself between us. He came
in for his own share of the scavenger-like fury of the
duke and peer. My servants interfered to separate us. I
had myself lost all restraint, and the blows were returned
as fast as they were given. We were now at the edge
of the staircase, where the bull fell, rolling over my servants, and dragging me along with him. This dreadful
shock restored him somewhat to himself. He heard a knock
at the street door, ran to it, saw the same young man * come
in, who had forewarned me that morning in my carriage; took
him by the arm, pushed him into the house, and swore that no
one should come in or go out, except by his order, until he had
torn me to pieces. Hearing the noise he was making, a crowd
had collected before the door; one of the women of the house
cried out from a window that her master was being assassinated.
My young friend, alarmed at seeing me thus disfigured and
covered with blood, wished to drag me up stairs. The duke
would not suffer it. His fury recommenced; he drew his sword,
which had remained at his side; for it must be remarked that
none of my people had yet dared to take it away from him,
thinking, as they afterwards informed me, it was a mark of
disrespect, which might have been attended with bad results
for them. He rushed upon me to run me through; eight persons fell upon him, and he was disarmed. He wounded my
valet in the head, cut my coachman's nose off, and ran my cook
through the hand. 'The treacherous coward,' I exclaimed;
'this is the second time he attacks me with a sword while
I am without arms.' He ran into the kitchen to look for
a knife; he was followed, and everything that could inflict a
mortal wound was put away. I armed myself with one of

* It was Gudin.

the fire-irons. I was about to come down, when I heard of a
thing which proved to me at once that this man had become
absolutely mad ; which was, that directly he no longer saw
me, he went into the dining-room, sat down by the table all
by himself, ate a large plateful of soup and some cutlets, and
drank two bottles of water. He heard another knock at the
street door, ran to open it, and saw M. Chenu, the Commissary of Police, who, surprised at the horrible disorder in
which he found all my servants, and startled, above all, by
my lacerated face, asked me what was the matter. 'The
matter is, Sir,' I replied, 'that a cowardly ruffian, who
came here with the intention of dining with me, sprang at
my face directly he had set foot in my room, and tried to
kill me with my own sword, and afterwards with his own.
You see, Sir, that with the persons I have about me, I might
have torn him to pieces ; but I should have had to give him
back better than he was before.' His relations, delighted to
have got rid of him, would, at the same time, have sought to
make it an awkward affair for me. I restrained myself, and,
with the exception of a hundred blows from my fist, with
which I replied to the outrage he had committed on my countenance and hair, I prevented any injury being done to him.'
The duke then spoke, and said, 'that he had had to fight me
at four o'clock, before M. le Comte de Turpin, who had been
chosen to act as witness, and that he had not been able to
wait until the hour agreed upon.' 'What do you think, Sir,
of this man, who, after committing a shameful outrage in my
house, himself divulges his guilty intention before a public
official, and destroys with one word all possibility of executing
his project, which this cowardice proves he had never seri-
ously contemplated?' At these words, my ruffian, who is as
brave with his fists as an English sailor, rushed a fifth time
upon me. I had laid by my improvised weapon on the arrival
of the commissary ; reduced to those of nature, I now defended myself, as best I could, before the assembly, which

separated us a third time. M. Chenu begged me to remain in my drawing-room, and took away the duke, who wanted to break the glasses. At this instant, my valet came back with a new sword; I took it and said to the commissary, 'Sir, I had no design to fight a duel,* nor shall I ever have one;' but without accepting a *rendez-vous* from this man, I shall go about the town with this sword constantly by my side, and if he insults me— as the publicity which he gives to this horrible adventure, proves, moreover, that he is the aggressor—I swear that if I can, the world which he disgraces by his baseness shall be delivered from him.' As the weapon which I then possessed was sufficiently imposing to inspire respect, he retired, without a word, into my dining-room, where M. Chenu, who followed him, was as surprised as he was frightened, to see him bruise his countenance with his fist, and tear out a handful of hair in each hand with rage, at his inability to kill me. M. Chenu at last prevailed upon him to go home, and he had the coolness to get his hair arranged by my valet, whom he had wounded. I went up stairs to get my wounds dressed, and he threw himself into his carriage."

After some other details, which it appeared useless to introduce, Beaumarchais terminates as follows :—

" I have introduced no reflection into this recital. I have stated the facts simply, and even have employed, as much as possible, the very expressions which were used, not wishing to give the slightest colouring to the truth, in narrating the strangest and most disgusting adventure which could happen to a reasonable man."

Now comes the report of the Commissary of Police

* The laws being still very strict against a duel, the Duke de Chaulnes will be seen to deny, on his side, that he ever intended to fight one.

to M. de Sartines. It will be noticed, above all towards the end, as one of the characteristics of the
period, with what reverential timidity a police magistrate, even in the exercise of his functions, spoke of
a. duke and peer who had conducted himself like a
scavenger, and how he seemed to fear giving any explanation in reference to him.

"Feb. 13, 1773.

"Sir,—You have asked me for the details of the affair
which took place between the Duke de Chaulnes and Le
Sieur de Beaumarchais, which I cannot give you very exactly, as I did not arrive at the house of the said Sieur de Beaumarchais until after the great disturbance was over. I found
M. le Duc de Chaulnes down stairs with his sword broken, having at his side nothing but a portion of the sheath. His hair
was untied, his coat and waistcoat were unbuttoned, and he
had no cravat. The Sieur de Beaumarchais was in an almost
similar state, and had moreover his black coat torn as well as
his shirt. He had no cravat, his hair was untied, and in the
greatest disorder, and his face was scratched in several places.
I prevailed upon these gentlemen to go up stairs, to a room
on the first floor, where they began again, said disagreeable
things to one another, and indulged reciprocally in somewhat
impolite reproaches, couched in very hard terms, which led to
their taking hold of one another again, and made me fear that
unfortunate consequences might come from it. I, however,
calmed M. le Duc a little, and invited him to pass into another
room, that we might talk together privately, which he consented to without difficulty. I made certain representations
to him in a civil manner on the subject of this scene. He
listened to them, and conformed to my request, which was
that nothing more should take place. This promise, he gives
me his word of honour that he kept; for whilst I went

out for about half a quarter of an hour, to speak of the matter to a cordon rouge,* who was dining in the quarter, and who had been named to me by the two parties, he went away from the house of the said Sieur de Beaumarchais. It is reported in public that M. le Duc de Chaulnes was rude to me, although he knew who I was. This fact is positively false; I have only praise to bestow on the conduct of M. le Duc, who *did not even say anything disagreeable to me,* but who, on the contrary, treated me with much civility, and *even* consideration.† In doing him this justice, I at the same time serve the cause of truth.

" I am, with respect, &c.,

" CHENU, Commissary."

The reader must be desirous of hearing the Duke de Chaulnes explain himself in his turn. We will append the deposition written and addressed by him to the Court of the Marshals of France. With the aid of the preceding documents it will be easy to discover in his narrative the points in regard to which he dissimulates or distorts facts. The style of this deposition, which I reproduce literally, has also its importance as a sign of the times.

" For more than three years," writes the Duke de Chaulnes, " I had the misfortune of being the dupe of M. de Beaumar-

---

* The Count de Turpin.

† Here the Commissary of Police adds, in a note—" *as well as the Sieur de Beaumarchais.*" It is somewhat curious to find this magistrate stating that the Duke de Chaulnes did " not *even* say anything disagreeable to him." That he " *even* showed him consideration," &c.

chais, whom I thought my friend, when valid reasons induced
me to keep him at a distance. It reached my ears several times
after this, that he had been in the habit of speaking very
ill of me. Finally, last Thursday, I found Le Sieur Gudin,
one of his friends, at the house of a woman of my acquaintance. He had the audacity * to assure her, on the part of Le
Sieur de Beaumarchais, that it was not true, as I had stated,
that a lady of quality had complained of his conduct. †
Wishing to have this contradiction explained, I went to look
for Le Sieur de Beaumarchais, at his own house, with Le Sieur
Gudin, whom I took in the same hackney-coach as myself, so
that he might not have time to prepare him. The Sieur de
Beaumarchais being at the Tribunal of the Captainry, I went
there and took him into a room apart, to tell him that I
wished for an explanation. So little was there any question of
it during the sitting, that I spoke to him about a game licence,
which he had promised to obtain for me at Orly. Count de
Marcouville and other officers of the Captainry were present.
On leaving the Captainry, I got into his carriage, and told the
coachman to go to M. de Turpin, who was connected with the
explanation I desired. M. de Turpin, who was going out, observed to us that it would be better to get into a hackney-coach
than to remain with three carriages collected at his door; that,
moreover, it was two o'clock, and that he only had a minute

---

* It is scarcely probable that Gudin had any kind of "audacity."

† This related to the subject already mentioned in Gudin's deposition, and which, if the unpublished manuscript is to be believed, related to some indiscretion of which Beaumarchais was falsely accused
in reference to a noble lady, the daughter of a Marshal of France,
whom Gudin does not name. It can be easily seen that the duke
does not choose to confess the real motive of his rage. He confesses
it, in another letter, to the Duke de la Vallière, in which he acknow-
lodges himself guilty of having allowed himself to be led away by a
" transport of jealous rage."

to spare, because he was expected at the Emperor's Embassy. Having got into the carriage, M. de Beaumarchais said to me, that in any case, I could not ask him for satisfaction, because he had only a mourning sword. I observed to him, that *if there were any question** of such a thing*, I was not better armed than himself, since I had only a small sword, without a guard: that I would, besides, change with him, if he desired it; but that, first of all, we wanted a more ample explanation. M. de Turpin observed again, that he was obliged to go away, which he did, with the understanding, that he was to come to my house at four. I went with M. de Beaumarchais to his house *to dine there;* † but hardly had he reached his room, when he began to address the most atrocious insults to me. I told him that he was an ill-bred person, and that he should come out immediately, and give me satisfaction in the street; but he preferred calling four of his people, who, with himself, threw themselves upon me and took my sword away.‡ He, at the same time, sent his sister for M. Chenu, the Commissary of Police, before whom he again dared to have the impudence to say to me, that I lied like a low scoundrel, and a thousand other horrible things. On leaving M. de Beaumarchais, I went and made my statement

---

* "If there were any question of it," is amusing; the duke, summoned before the tribunal of the Marshals of France, does not like to avow that he has challenged Beaumarchais.

† "To dine there," is charming in its *naïveté*, after the conversation with Gudin in the hackney coach, in which the duke says he wishes to tear Beaumarchais' heart out with his teeth.

‡ Beaumarchais' account is ten times more probable, and completely destroys this statement of the duke's, who, moreover, destroys himself in the next phrase; for, if Beaumarchais had intended to have the duke knocked down by four of his people, what interest could he have had in sending at the same time for the Commissary of Police?

to M. de Sartines, and the next day but one afterwards, by his advice, to M. de la Vrillière. On returning from Versailles, I learnt that Le Sieur de Beaumarchais was retailing the story to my disparagement, saying, that he had challenged me, and that I had refused to follow him. In order to destroy, in a positive manner, all mystery about this point, I thought it best (many serious persons thought the same) to go to the lobbies of the theatres, and say, that as M. de Beaumarchais was stating things against my honour, and was not of noble birth, he did not deserve that I should compromise myself as I had done the day before, but should be corrected like a plebeian. Since this time, the Sieur de Beaumarchais has been at liberty four days without my hearing anything of him. It would have been difficult to know that he was of noble birth as he is the son of a watchmaker; he does not even appear in the 'Royal Almanac' as King's Secretary,[*] and it was not even known at the court, for a long time, whether he was eligible. Altogether, if the majority of the facts of this affair could not be verified as easily as they can, even if the insults which M. de Beaumarchais had the impudence to address to me before the Commissary himself, did not afford a strong presumption of what he might say and do in the absence of witnesses, it would be sufficient for me to remind persons that I have never been known to a law-court, to the police, in Paris, or in any place, as a quarrelsome person, a gambler, or a madman, while the reputation of M. de Beaumarchais is far from being equally intact; for, independently of his well-known insolence, and the most incredible rumours, *he is at this moment undergoing a criminal prosecution for forgery.*"

This last phrase of the Duke de Chaulnes is a gross

[*] All the preceding passage is very significant in style. The last assertion of the duke is incorrect. I have not been able to test it by the Almanac of 1773, but I have found the name of Beaumarchais in several Almanacs of an earlier date.

calumny, for he knew perfectly well that *Beaumarchais was not undergoing a criminal prosecution for forgery*, but that he was engaged in a civil action with the Count de la Blache on the subject of a deed of which he disputed the genuineness, without ever daring to prosecute him directly for forgery. We can, however, see by this what a disastrous influence this action with La Blache exercised on Beaumarchais' reputation, since the Duke de Chaulnes did not fear, during the very time of the action, to distort facts in so revolting a manner. The fact of the duke doing thus the honours of his adversary's morality, obliges us to remind the reader that he himself was at this time bringing an action of a horribly scandalous nature against his own mother; that the documents beneath our eyes prove that he was as debauched and disorderly in every way, as he was brutal; and that, after being banished from the kingdom for acts of violence, his entire life was but a series of acts of the same nature.

The day of the 11th of February having been so stormy, it would be natural to think that Beaumarchais employed the evening in regaining his tranquillity, in repose, and in taking precautions for the next day: however, if I am to believe Gudin's manuscript, as he was expected the same evening at the house of one of his friends, to read " The Barber of Seville " to a numerous party, he arrived at the

rendezvous fresh and ready—at least morally so—
read his comedy with much *verve*, gave a lively
account of the furious behaviour of the Duke de
Chaulnes, and passed a portion of the night in playing the harp and singing seguedillas. "Thus," says
Gudin, "in every circumstance of his life he was entirely devoted to whatever occupied his attention,
without being turned away from it either by what
had taken place, or by what was to follow, so sure
was he of his own faculties and of his presence of
mind. He never needed preparation on any point;
his intelligence was at his command at all times, and
his principles were never at fault."

The next morning Gudin tells us how old M.
Caron brought his son an old sword of the time of
his youth, and said to him, "You young men have
now only indifferent arms; here is a substantial one,
and of a time when people fought more often than
than they do in the present day: take it; and if that
scoundrel of a duke approaches you, kill him like a
mad dog." However, the duel was no longer possible; the Duke de Chaulnes had thought fit to go to
the lobbies of all the theatres, and declare openly
that, as his rival was not a nobleman, he should correct him like a plebeian. The altercation having thus
been made public, the Tribunal of the Marshals of
France, which decided cases of this kind between
noblemen—(and, without wishing to contradict the

Duke de Chaulnes, Beaumarchais was one, it will be remembered, in virtue of his *receipt*)—the tribunal of the Marshals took up the affair, and sent a guard to each of the two adversaries.

During the interval the Duke de la Vrillière, minister of the king's household, had summoned Beaumarchais, and ordered him to retire to the country for some days; and as he protested energetically against such an order—the compliance with which, immediately after the threats of the Duke de Chaulnes, would have compromised his honour—the minister had directed him to remain under arrest at his own house, until he had rendered an account of this conflict to the king. It was at this juncture that the Tribunal of the Marshals of France successively called the two contending parties before it.   Beaumarchais had no trouble in proving that all his crime consisted in being preferred to a duke and peer by a pretty woman, in possession of her liberty, which was not a capital offence; and the result of the inquiry having been unfavourable to the Duke de Chaulnes, the latter was sent on the 19th of February, by a *lettre de cachet*, to the château of Vincennes. The tribunal of the Marshals of France having summoned Beaumarchais a second time, informed him that he was free, and no longer under arrest.

All this was sufficiently just; but Beaumarchais, who was rather distrustful of human justice, called upon the Duke de la Vrillière, to know whether he was really to consider himself at liberty. Not finding him at home, he left a message for him, and then went straight to M. de Sartines to put the same question to him. The lieutenant of police replied that he was perfectly free. Then, and not till then, he considered himself secure from all accident, and ventured into the streets of Paris. He had reckoned without his host; the very little mind of the Duke de la Vrillière was offended at the Tribunal of the Marshals of France rescinding "in the name of the king," an order of arrest which had been imposed by him "in the name of the king;" and, in order to teach this tribunal to pay more regard to his authority, sent Beaumarchais on the 24th of February, still "in the name of the king," to For-l'Evêque. Perhaps, also, he was made to perceive that it was unbecoming to send a duke and peer to Vincennes, while the son of a watchmaker got off with having merely to repair, as best he could, the damage done to his countenance by the duke and peer's violence.

CHAPTER X.

BEAUMARCHAIS, then, was taken away from his family,
his occupation, his law-suit, and imprisoned, contrary
to all justice. At another period such an act of
iniquity would not have passed without notice; but
the public then took but little interest in the man
who was shortly to become its idol. "This individual," said "Bachaumont's Miscellany," speaking
of "The Barber of Seville," and of the adventures
we are relating, "this very insolent* individual, who

* It must be remarked that, if some persons reproved Beaumarchais
with being too insolent, others, and especially Dumouriez, who was
then very intimate with him, considered that he had not shown

has so much self-assurance, is not liked; and although in this quarrel it does not appear that there is any thing to reproach him with, he is pitied less than another person would be for the vexations he has experienced."

Beaumarchais' first letter from his prison is philosophic enough; it is addressed to Gudin.

"In virtue" he writes, "of a *lettre sans cachet*,* called *lettre de cachet*, signed Louis, and lower down, Phelippaux, recommended Sartines, executed Buchot, and undergone Beaumarchais, I have been domiciled, my friend, since this morning at For-l'Evêque, in a room without carpet, at a rent of 2160 livres, where I am given to hope that, beyond necessaries, I shall want nothing. Is it the duke's family which I have saved from a criminal prosecution, that imprisons me? Is it the minister, whose orders I have constantly followed or anticipated? Is it the dukes and peers, with whom I can never have anything to do? That I cannot say; but the sacred name of the king is such a fine thing, that it cannot be too much repeated and made use of. It is thus

---

enough anxiety to meet the Duke de Chaulnes again, the day after the scene. (*Vide* Appendix No. 1—a letter which Dumouriez wrote to Beaumarchais several years afterwards to acknowledge his error, and apologise for having spoken badly of him in the Chaulnes affair). Beaumarchais might have replied to his detractors, that there was more than one danger for him to overcome, the family of the duke being very powerful.

* This pleasantry, which Beaumarchais repeats in his Memorials against Goëzman, is explained by the fact that the *lettres de cachet*, which were also called *lettres closes*, differed from other royal missives, in so far that they only bore the king's sign-manual, and were not sealed with the great seal of state.

that, in all well-regulated countries, those who cannot be inculpated with justice, are punished by authority! What can be done? Wherever there are men, odious things take place; and the great wrong of being right is always a crime in the eyes of power, which wishes incessantly to punish and never to judge."

Whilst the two rivals are under lock and key, given up to the reflections engendered by solitude, and meditating on the inconveniences of friendship between persons in disproportionate positions, let us pay a little attention to Mademoiselle Ménard. On hearing of the Duke de Chaulnes' fit of rage, this fair Helen had gone and thrown herself at the feet of M. de Sartines, to implore his protection. The polite magistrate had re-assured her as well as he could; the day afterwards she wrote him this letter :—

" Sir,—In spite of the proofs of kindness you exhibited towards me in granting me your protection, I cannot conceal from you my alarm and fear; the disposition of the violent man I am flying from is too well known to me, not to make me dread a future which will be as fatal to him as to me. In order to save myself from it, and preserve him from his fits of jealousy, I have positively resolved to enter a convent. Whatever may be my place of refuge, I shall have the honour to inform you of it. I venture to beg that to him it may be inaccessible. This important benefit will add to the gratitude which I feel beforehand for your offers to serve me. I rely so much upon them, that under the shelter of your name and authority I have already placed my daughter in the convent of the Presentation, where M. l'Abbé Dugué did me the pleasure of taking her this very evening. Deign to grant your protection equally to the mother and the child, who, after God, place all their trust in you—a trust which is only equalled by the respectful sentiments with which I have the honour to be, Sir, your very humble and very obedient servant,

"MENARD."

The following day came a fresh letter, in which Mademoiselle Ménard persisted in her project of entering a convent. "Weary," she said, "of being his victim (the Duke de Chaulnes'), and of making myself the plaything of the public, I fortified myself more and more in my resolution to accept the convent as my lot." Only in reading over her letter, Mademoiselle Ménard experiences a slight scruple of conscience, and adds at the bottom of the page, by means of a note referring to the word "lot," these words, "at least for some time." She evidently feared that M. de Sartines would form too great a notion of the irresistible nature of her vocation. This magistrate sent for the Abbé Dugué, of whom we have just spoken, and commissioned him to find a convent for Mademoiselle Ménard. That very evening, the abbé told him how he had fulfilled his mission, in a letter which appears interesting to me. This letter is not from a frivolous priest, such as we should naturally imagine an abbé of the eighteenth century employed by M. de Sartines in an affair of this kind to be. It is from a very estimable man, very kind, and very simple-hearted. Somewhat embarrassed with the part he is made to play, afraid of compromising his character he is also very much afraid, like Gudin, and the commissary of police, of incurring the hostility of a duke and peer; the more so, as the Duke de Chaulnes had not yet been sent to prison when the Abbé Dugué wrote to M. de Sartines in these terms :—

" February 15, 1773.

" Monseigneur,*—After the audience you granted me, I repaired to the convent of the Presentation, to see, in accordance with your orders, whether a retreat could not be found there for both mother and child—I speak of Mademoiselle Ménard and her little girl, whom I had conducted to this monastery on Thursday evening, as I had the honour to inform you last Saturday. I was unable to succeed; there was absolutely no place; and certainly, with your recommendation and the good wishes of the prioress towards this lady, she would have been well received if there had been any room. Being unsuccessful here, I returned to the Cordelières of the Rue de l'Oursine, faubourg Saint-Marceau, and after many questions, which I was obliged to reply to or evade, I received, on Sunday morning, in reference to my application yesterday, a letter of reception; in consequence of which I this day, at about eleven in the morning, conducted Mademoiselle Ménard to the convent of the Cordelières. Can I venture to confess to you, Monseigneur, that, mixed up innocently enough in this catastrophe, which may have unfortunate consequences, and hearing more than I like of the violent intentions of the person from whom Mademoiselle Ménard is taking refuge, I

---

* The lieutenant of police was not addressed as " Monseigneur," but the good abbé did not mind that.

much fear that my too great kindness may be made the subject of very injurious reproaches.   One thing alone could reassure me, which was the knowledge that it was possible to prevent M. le Duke de Ch—— or M. de B—— and their agents—for such they have—to invade this asylum; for, considering the difficulties which were made about receiving the young lady, whom in my anxiety to get rid of, however, I had to represent as my relation, and free from reproach, what effect will it have upon me in my profession, if through the violence, or even imprudence of either of the persons interested, these nuns discover the real character of the person I have introduced to them? . . .   Whilst, on the other hand, if these hasty rivals could allow her to remain tranquil, the fact of all passing quietly, joined to the sweetness of countenance, and still more of the disposition of this afflicted recluse, would do everything in her favour in this religious establishment, and would prevent my passing not only for a liar, but even for a person who countenances irregular conduct.   I left these ladies very well disposed towards their new boarder; but, I repeat, what a disgrace for her and for me, who have advanced so far, if jealousy or love, equally out of place, should reach her parlour, to breathe forth their scandalous transports, or their unedifying sighs.*

Mademoiselle Ménard had commissioned me to communicate to you some other details respecting her; a letter cannot contain them; the present one is already only too importunate.   If what concerns her in the present circumstances, interests you sufficiently to authorise me to speak to you again about her, deign in that case to tell me at what moment I shall satisfy you.   In obeying your orders, I shall respond to the singular confidence which she has placed in me.   May

---

* Is not this Abbé Dugué a very worthy man, with his "unedifying sighs?" M. de Sartines and Beaumarchais, both much less ingenuous, must have smiled a little on reading this passage.

my feeble services, without compromising myself, alleviate her troubles.

"I am with respect, Monsiegneur, your very humble and very obedient servant,

"DUGUE the Elder, Priest,

"Cloister of Notre-Dame."

This "afflicted recluse," as the good abbé says, was not made for the life of a convent; she had scarcely tasted this kind of existence for a fortnight, when she already felt the necessity of varying her impressions, and returned suddenly to the world, tranquillised otherwise by the solidity of the walls of the Château de Vincennes, which separated her from the Duke de Chaulnes. Then came the interference of Beaumarchais, who had much approved of the convent project, and who, while he was shut up by authority at For-l'Evêque, thought it wrong that Mademoiselle Ménard should have no inclination for a life of seclusion. He addressed the following letter to her through the medium of M. de Sartines.

"No person has a right to interfere with the liberty of another; but the counsels of friendship should acquire increased weight in proportion to their disinterestedness. I hear, Mademoiselle, that you have left the convent as suddenly as you entered it. What can be your motives for an action which appears so imprudent? Did you fear lest some abuse of authority should keep you there? Reflect, I beg of you, whether you are more secure in your own house from being carried off and placed in a convent, if some powerful enemy should consider himself strong enough to keep you there. Any disquietude which may be given you on this subject is illusory, or springs from interested motives. What happiness can you find in moving incessantly from one place to another, and what attraction can that horrible residence, in which you have suffered so much, have for you? In the distressing situation of your affairs, after having, perhaps, exhausted your purse by paying for a quarter's board in advance, and furnished an apartment in the convent, ought you without necessity to triple your expenses? and is not the voluntary retreat to which you had been led by fear and grief, a hundred times more suitable an asylum during the first moments of trouble, than the horrible residence from which you ought to wish to be at a hundred leagues distance? I hear that you weep! What do you weep for? Are you the cause of M. de Chaulnes' misfortune and my own? You are only the pretext; and if, in this execrable adventure, any one has thanks to offer to fate, it is you, who, without having anything to reproach yourself with, have recovered that liberty which the most unjust of tyrants and madmen had arrogated the right of invading. I ought also to take account of what you owe to this good and kind Abbé Dugué, who, to serve you, was obliged to conceal your name and your troubles in the convent where you were received on his representations. Does not your departure, which looks like a sally of caprice, compromise him with his superiors, by making him appear to have mixed himself up in a dark intrigue, while he has throughout shown nothing but kindness, zeal, and compassion for you? You are good and kind, but so many repeated shocks may have produced disorder in your ideas. It would be well if some prudent person were to take upon himself to show you your position, exactly as it is, not a happy but a calm one. Believe me, my dear friend, return to the convent, where you are said to have gained general affection. While you remain there, break yourself of the useless and expensive mode of life which you lead, contrary to all reason. The notion, which is attributed to you of re-appearing on the stage is an insane one; you must only think of tranquillizing your head and re-establishing your health. Finally, Mademoiselle, whatever may be your ideas for the future, they cannot, and ought not to be indifferent to me. I must be informed of them; and I venture to say to you, that I am, perhaps, the only man from whom you can accept assistance without blushing. The more it is proved by your remaining in the convent that we have no intimate relations, the more I shall be entitled to declare myself your friend, your protector, your brother, and your adviser.

"BEAUMARCHAIS."

Beaumarchais, however, soon resigned himself to Mademoiselle Ménard's freedom; she was more useful to him at liberty than in her convent, for she interceded energetically for him, and it appears that she had not failed to acquire a certain influence over M. de Sartines.

As for Beaumarchais himself, who, on the first day of his captivity, appeared to have resigned himself to his fate with sufficient philosophy, he was now horribly annoyed; his incarceration occurring as it did in the middle of his action against the Count de la Blache, did him fearful injury; his adversary, profiting by the circumstance, laboured incessantly to blacken his character in the opinion of the judge; took all sorts of steps; obtained the recommendations and solicitations of influential persons, and pressed eagerly for the case to be decided, while the unfortunate prisoner whose fortune and honour were engaged in this affair could not even manage to obtain permission to go out for a few hours, in order that he, in his turn, might visit his judges. M. de Sartines showed the greatest kindness to him, but he could only alleviate his position; his liberty depended on the minister. Beaumarchais had commenced by representing his case to the Duke de la Vrillière, as that of a citizen unjustly imprisoned. He sent him memorials upon memorials, containing superabundant proof that he had done no wrong. He demanded to be informed the reason of his detention; and when M. de Sartines warned him, in a friendly manner, that this tone would lead to nothing, he replied with haughtiness—"The only satisfaction of the persecuted is to testify that they are persecuted unjustly."

Whilst exhausting himself in vain protests, the period for the decision of his law-suit drew near; to M. de Sartines' request that he might be allowed to go out for some hours in the day, the Duke de la Vrillière replied, without writing—"This man is too insolent; let him leave the conduct of his affair to his solicitor." Thereupon Beaumarchais, with despair and indignation, wrote to M. de Sartines in these words:—

"It has been clearly proved to me now, that I am intended to lose my suit, if it is a suit that can be lost, or about which there is even a doubt : but I confess to you that I was not prepared for the derisive observation of the Duke de la Vrillière, who tells me to 'leave the representations connected with my affair to my solicitor:' when he knows as well as I do, that solicitors are not allowed to make them. Great gods! can they not ruin an innocent man without laughing in his face? * Thus I have been grievously insulted, and justice has been denied me, because my adversary is a man of quality. I have been put in prison, and I am kept there, because I have been insulted by a man of quality! People go so far as to find fault with me for correcting the public of the false impressions it has received, while the shameless 'Gazette de Deux-ponts,' and 'Gazette de Hollande,' libel me in a scandalous manner, in order to serve my adversary of quality. A little more, and I should have been told that I was very insolent, to be insulted in every possible manner by a man of quality ; for what does the phrase mean, which is considered a sufficient answer for all persons interceding in my behalf: 'He has made too much fuss about the affair?' Could I do less than ask for justice, and prove, from the actions of my adversary, that I was not to blame? What a pretext for ruining and destroying an injured man, to say, 'He has talked about the affair too much;' as if it were possible for me to speak of anything else! Receive my thanks, Sir, for having communicated to me this refusal and this remark of M. la Vrillière's, and for the happiness of this country, may your power be one day equal to your wisdom and your integrity !

* I have said elsewhere that Beaumarchais was a Pagan in love. He was a Pagan, to some extent, in everything, without being aware of it ; for he here writes quite naturally, "great gods!" in the plural, as Horace or Tibullus might exclaim—" Dii immortales ! "

There will then be no need of petitions for unhappy men to present. My gratitude is equal to the profound respect with which

" I am, &c.,

" BEAUMARCHAIS.

" March 11, 1773."

I have said that Mademoiselle Ménard was joining her solicitations to those of Beaumarchais. Let us quote, in reference to this subject, another letter from the prisoner to M. de Sartines, which appears to us rather *piquante,* both in details and form :—

" At For-l'Evêque, March 20, 1773.

" Sir,—M. the Duke de la Vrillière said to Choisy last week, that I ought to know why I was in prison, as he had told me in his letter. The truth is, that I have received neither letter nor note from any one on the subject of my detention. I am allowed the privilege of guessing the cause if I can, according to the custom of the Roman Inquisition.

" Madame Ménard only told me yesterday, through one of her friends, that you had kindly promised her to make a fresh effort with the minister in my favour, next Sunday; but the mysterious manner in which the information was given to me, might almost make me doubt its truth; for the good little girl conveyed it with all the pretty and puerile *mignardises* with which her sex season their slightest favours. If I am to believe her, it is necessary to have a special order to see me, witnesses to accompany her, permissions to write to me, and even to take precautions in venturing to correspond with me by means of a third party. Through all this, however, *agnosco veteris vestigia flammæ,* and I cannot help smiling at this mixture of childishness and kindly interest. The idea of persuading me that the minister does me the favour to pay the most severe attention, even to my intimacies! Does the tennis player in handling the balls inquire of what the interior is made?

However this may be, Sir, I renew my anxious prayers that you will call the attention of the minister to the fearful injury which may result to me from not making a personal solicitation in the La Blache case, and I offer you my most sincere thanks, if you have, indeed, had the kindness to promise Madame Ménard to do so.

" I venture to hope that you will not tell this excellent little woman that I have informed you of the importance which she pretends is attached to the frivolous steps she takes in so important an affair, in which the question is no less a one than that of the detention of a citizen, who has been insulted, grievously insulted, who is a plaintiff not yet heard, and who is thrown by the authorities into prison, and left there to rot and be ruined.

" The more this amiable child endeavours to make me believe, the less would she pardon me for doubting what she says, above all for informing you of it, and as Ovid or Propertius says, *nullæ sunt inimicitiæ nisi amoris acerbæ;* but I perceive that in blaming her, I behave like herself, and that I indiscreetly mix up trifling matters with the most serious requests. I stop, and am with the most profound respect, Sir, your very humble and obedient servant,

"BEAUMARCHAIS."

This correspondence, in which Beaumarchais associated Virgil, Ovid, Propertius, and Mademoiselle Ménard, in defence of his citizen's rights, doubtless amused M. de Sartines, but it in no way advanced the interests of the prisoner. What the Duke de la Vrillière required from him, before everything,

was, that he should cease to be insolent, that is to
say, to ask for justice, and that he should make
up his mind to ask for pardon.   He had held up
for nearly a month, until the 20th of March, when,
on that very day he received a long letter, without a signature, written by a man who appeared
to take a great interest in him, and who endeavoured to make him understand that, under an
absolute government, when the disgrace of a
minister has been incurred, when this minister is
keeping you in prison, and when you have the
greatest interest in getting out of prison, the thing
is not to plead in the character of an oppressed
citizen, but to submit to the law of might, and
assume the character of the supplicant.   What was
Beaumarchais to do?   He was on the point of losing
a law-suit of the greatest importance to his fortune
and honour; his liberty was in the hands of a man
who was personally far from estimable, for the Duke
de la Vrillière is one of the ministers most -justly despised in history; but the situation was such that this
man could dispose of his destiny as he thought fit.
Beaumarchais at last became resigned and humbled
himself; here we have him in the position of a supplicant:—

"Monseigneur,—The dreadful affair of the Duke de
Chaulnes has resulted for me in a chain of misfortunes without end, and the greatest of all is that of having incurred your

displeasure; but if, in spite of the purity of my inten- tions, the grief by which I am distracted has carried me away, and induced me to take steps which may have dis- pleased you, I disavow them at your feet, Monseigneur, and beg you to grant me your generous pardon; or if I appear to you to deserve a longer term of imprisonment, permit me only to go out for some days, in order to instruct my judges with regard to an affair which is of the greatest importance to my fortune and honour, and after its decision I will submit with gratitude to whatever punishment you may im- pose upon me. The whole of my family, in tears, join their prayers to mine. Every one, Monseigneur, praises your in- dulgence and the goodness of your heart. Shall I be the only one to implore you in vain? By a single word, you can over- whelm a multitude of honest persons with joy, whose lively gratitude will equal the very profound respect with which we are all, and myself especially, Monseigneur,

"Yours, &c.,

"CARON DE BEAUMARCHAIS.

"At For-l'Evêque, March 21, 1773."

The Duke de la Vrillière was satisfied in his paltry vanity; accordingly, he did not delay sending an an- swer. The next day, March 22, the minister for- warded to M. de Sartines an authorization allowing the prisoner to go out, under the conduct of a police agent, obliging him at the same time to return to For-l'Evêque to sleep.*

In case the reader should happen not to consider Beaumarchais sufficiently heroic, I will observe that the Duke de Chaulnes, imprisoned, on his side, at

* See the minister's order, Appendix No. 2.

Vincennes, whose correspondence is also beneath my
eyes, was not more so.   By a somewhat strange co-
incidence, he also had a law-suit to follow up, and
affairs to transact, and his letters to the Duke de la
Vrillière are not less plaintive than those of Beaumarchais.   Like the latter he is allowed to go out
under the conduct of a police agent, on condition
that he will leave his rival in peace, and will not go
to see Mademoiselle Ménard contrary to her wishes.
The person charged with surveillance of all these
"important interests" is M. de Sartines, who receives
simultaneously the alternately facetious and. despond-
dent notes of Beaumarchais, and the "unedifying
sighs" of the Duke de Chaulnes.

As the duke first of all appeared to us under a disagreeable aspect, it is just that, before separating from
him for ever, we should look in his correspondence
for some testimony in his favour.   He used to beat
Mademoiselle Ménard, it is true; he tore Gudin's
wig off, and had a fight with Beaumarchais: all that
is not very aristocratic; but here are two notes from
him, addressed to M. de Sartines, in which a basis of
resigned sadness and generosity can be discovered,
to reconcile us a little to this violent and wild
being.

"I heard, Sir, on coming home, where Madame Ménard
was. I will keep my word with you, and will only go to see her
with her own consent. I promise you, moreover, that nothing

shall happen between M. de Beaumarchais and myself, if you will have him instructed to keep himself at the distance from me, which he has voluntarily kept himself for the last two days. I think, however, I can arrange so as to leave in a month or six weeks. I hope Madame Ménard will be kind enough to wait until then, to live with M. de Beaumarchais, and that she will only inform me of it through you, if such should be her permanent intention after what will have taken place in the interval.

"I have the honour to be, truly, Sir, your very humble and very obedient servant,

."THE DUKE DE CHAULNES.

"Tuesday Morning."

The second note proves, at the same time, the generosity of the duke, (although it perhaps proceeded somewhat from self-interest,) and the extreme complaisance of M. de Sartines, who transformed himself into a postman for the benefit of Mademoiselle Ménard.

"You have with much kindness, Sir, rendered me all the services in your power; may I venture to ask, as an additional one, that you will convey this letter to Madame Ménard? The object of that of the Duke de Luxembourg's was to provide for her future; that of the present one, is to inform her of it in a direct manner. Uneasiness respecting the fate of a very dear friend, would be too great a misfortune to add to those which overwhelm me, for me not to hope that you will make allowances for it, and that you will give me this mark of your friendship, which will have the effect of increasing, if it be possible to do so, my gratitude, and the very perfect attachment with which I have the honour to be, Sir, &c.,

"THE DUKE DE CHAULNES.

"Wednesday."

Some readers will be sufficiently curious, perhaps, to inquire what became of the seductive actress, who had been the cause of this great quarrel. I must avow, humbly, that I do not know. Mademoiselle Ménard disappears from the papers of Beaumarchais, who had something else to do besides thinking, to use the Duke de Chaulnes terms, of "living with her." In some news-sheets of a much later date, which came by chance beneath my notice, she is spoken of as a woman who at last entitled herself to the somewhat severe epithet which La Harpe gave her, without being acquainted with her. However, as these *feuilles à la main,* are not articles of faith, we will leave Mademoiselle Ménard in the medium position, between the honest woman and the courtesan, which is assigned to her with mathematical precision by the excellent abbé Dugué.

Let us return to Beaumarchais, who profited by his half-liberty to go, as was the custom then, and solicit his judges. Before showing how he lost his law-suit, let me be allowed to extract once more from his prison correspondence, a somewhat graceful little incident in which he appears in a very pleasing light. I have elsewhere stated that he was on an intimate footing with M. Lenormant D'Etioles, the husband of Madame de Pompadour, who, after the death of his first wife, had married again, and who had a charming child six years and a half old. This little boy, who was named Constant, was very fond of Beaumarchais, and on hearing that his friend was in prison, he wrote to him, of his own accord, the following letter :—

> "Neuilly, March 2, 1773.
>
> "SIR,—I send you my purse, because people in prison are always poor. I am very sorry you are in prison. Every morning and every evening I say an Ave Maria for you.
>
> "I have the honour to be, Sir,
>
> Your very humble and very obedient servant,
>
> "CONSTANT."

Beaumarchais replied immediately to the mother and child by two letters, in which all his good nature and delicacy of feeling are shown. Here is, first of all, his letter to Madame Lenormant :—

> "I thank you very sincerely, Madame, for having conveyed to me the letter and purse of my little friend Constant. These are the first promptings of benevolence on the part of a young nature, from which excellent things may be expected. Do not give him back his own purse, so that he may not conclude that all sacrifices bring with them this species of reward. It will be very gratifying to him one day to see it in your hands, as a memorial of the affectionate kindness of his generous heart. Compensate him in a manner which will give him a just idea of the nature of his action, without allowing himself to become proud of having done it. But I do not know what I am saying when I make these observations.

Your care has originated and developed in him so great a quality as that of beneficence at an age when all morality consists in referring things to one's own interest. Receive my thanks and compliments. Allow M. l'Abbé Leroux * to share them; he is not contented with teaching his pupils to decline the word virtue, he also teaches them to love it; he is full of merit, and more fitted than any other man to second your views. This letter and this purse have produced quite a child's delight in myself. Happy parents! you have a son six years of age capable of such an action. And I also had a son; but he is no more! And yours already gives you such pleasures! I share them with all my heart, and I beg that you will continue to have a little affection for him who has been the cause of this charming trait on the part of our little Constant. Nothing can be added to the respectful attachment of him who makes it his honour to be, Madame, &c.

"At For-l'Evêque, March 4, 1773."

Now comes the answer to little Constant:—

"My little Friend Constant,—I have received with much gratitude your letter and the purse you added to it; I have made a just division of what they contained, according to the different wants of my fellow prisoners and myself, keeping the best portion for your friend Beaumarchais, I mean the prayers, the Aves, of which I have certainly great need, and distributing to poor people, who were in distress, all the money your purse contained. Thus, while intending to oblige one man only, you have earned the gratitude of many. This is the ordinary fruit of actions like yours. Good-bye, my little friend Constant,

"BEAUMARCHAIS."

This is the man whom the Count la Blache chari-

---

* This was little Constant's preceptor.

tably entitled a "finished monster," a "venomous species of being, of which society ought and must be purged;" and at the time the count spoke thus, his opinion was almost universally adopted. It was in vain that Beaumarchais, followed by his guard, and coming back every evening to prison, passed the day in running about to the residences of his judges; the discredit which was then attached to his name followed him everywhere. Under the influence of this discredit, and on the report of the Councillor Goëzman, the Parliament decided at length between him and M. de La Blache, and, April 6, 1773, gave a judgment which was extraordinary, in a legal point of view; this judgment, overruling that of the lower court, declared to be null and void an act which had been signed of their own free will, by two majors, without any necessity existing, said the sentence, "for letters of rescision;" that is to say, that the question of fraud, surprise, or error, being put on one side, Beaumarchais found himself declared indirectly a forger, although there was no accusation of forgery against him. And in order that no doubt might exist as to the meaning of the decision, it was subsequently explained as follows, by the judge Goëzman, who had induced the decision, and who will soon appear as the personal adversary of the litigant whom he had already sacrificed. "The Parliament," he said, "has thereby decided, not exactly that the engage-

E 2

ments which this writing appeared to attribute to
M. Pâris du Verney, were the effect of fraud, surprise, or error, but that they were certainly not made
by M. du Verney; in one word, that the writing
which appears above the signature, has been produced without his having had anything to do with it;
and as M. Caron admits that this writing is entirely
in his hand, it follows that he is declared to have
fabricated a fraudulent document." While this decision disgraced Beaumarchais, it at the same time
gave a heavy blow to his fortune. The Parliament
had not dared to give M. de La Blache, as he had
demanded, all the claims, which appeared in the
statement of accounts declared null: the injustice
would have been too flagrant; but it condemned his
adversary to pay the 56,300 livres of debts which
the statement of accounts annulled, the interest
on these debts for five years, and the expenses
of the action. Beaumarchais exaggerates a little in
his Memorials against Goëzman, when he says the
action cost him 50,000 crowns; it cost him less, but
sufficient to crush him, particularly as at the very
moment when the Count de la Blache seized all
his goods and income, other pretended creditors, with
no more real claims than the count, but enticed by
his success, united their prosecutions to his; and this
man, attacked by so many disasters at once, obliged
to make head against them all, and to support his

father, his sisters, and his nieces, petitioned with the greatest earnestness, but in vain, that his prison doors might be opened.

" My courage is exhausted," he writes, April 9, 1773, to M. de Sartines. " The public report is, that I am entirely sacrificed; my credit has fallen, my affairs have been ruined, my family, of whom I am the father and the support, is in the greatest distress. Sir, I have done good throughout my life, without ostentation, and have always been torn to pieces by the wicked. If you were acquainted with the interior of my home, you would see that, as a good son, a good brother, a good husband, and a useful citizen, I have collected nothing but blessings around me; while abroad, I have been calumniated without shame. Whatever revenge may be taken upon me for this miserable affair of the Duke de Chaulnes, is it not to have some bounds? It is fully proved that my imprisonment costs me 100,000 francs. The substance, the form, everything in this unjust decision, causes shudders, and I cannot recover from its effects, as long as I am kept in a horrible prison. I have sufficient strength to resist my own misfortunes; I have none to oppose to the tears of my worthy father, who is seventy-five years old, and who is dying from grief at the abject condition into which I have fallen; I have none against the grief of my sisters and nieces, who are already terrified by the poverty in store for them, owing to the state in which my detention has thrown me personally, and the disorder into which it has plunged my affairs. All the activity of my mind turns now against myself; my situation is killing me; I am struggling against an acute disease, of which I feel the premonitory symptoms in inability to sleep and distaste for every kind of food; the atmosphere of my prison is infected, and is destroying my wretched health."

The reader sees that there is no exaggeration in

the eloquent pages of the Memorials against Goëzman, in which, at a later period, Beaumarchais represents his situation in prison. They are but a more
ornate reproduction of the complaints this situation
draws from him in the unpublished letter we have
just given.

The minister, La Vrillière, was at last moved, and
on the 8th May, 1773, after an imprisonment of two
months and a half, without cause, restored the prisoner to liberty. And now from this law-suit, which
he lost, arises a new, a more terrible law-suit, which
was calculated to complete Beaumarchais' ruin, but
which saved him, which made him pass, in a few
months, from a state of dejection and misfortune,
in which, to employ his own expressions, he felt
shame and pity for himself, to that of a man
triumphing over a parliament, and the favourite of
an entire nation. "He was," said Grimm, "the
horror of all Paris a year since; every one, upon the
mere word of his neighbour, thought him capable of
the greatest crimes: at present every one is full of his
virtues." It remains to us to explain how this revul-
sion in opinion took place.

CHAPTER XI.

THE PARLIAMENTS AND THE THRONE IN THE EIGH-
TEENTH CENTURY.—GOVERNMENT OF LOUIS XIV.—
THE DUKE AND THE BOURGEOIS.—THE PARLIAMENT
OF LOUIS XV.—OFFICIAL ANARCHY.—THE MAUPEOU
PARLIAMENT. — BEAUMARCHAIS' ACTION AGAINST
GOEZMAN.

THE Goëzman law-suit opens the brilliant period
of Beaumarchais' life. By turns a courtier, a speculator, and a playwright, the son of Caron the
watchmaker, in all these different paths, had, as
yet, only met with doubtful, disputed success, and
the most ardent enmity. He was at last about
to conquer fortune and regain a lengthened popularity, and to associate his name with an important fact in the history of our country.

What was the subject of this famous quarrel between Beaumarchais and the Councillor Goëzman?
It all depended upon whether the wife of a judge had
or had not received fifteen louis from one of the
parties to a suit. To understand how a debate of so
little importance to himself, could for a moment
agitate the whole of France, assume the proportions

of an historic event, contribute to the downfall of a parliament, and the failure of a *coup d'état*, it is necessary, first of all, to take into account the situation of affairs at the moment when this law-suit was occupying public attention.

The history of government in France, during the eighteenth century, presents an analogy with Beaumarchais' life, in so far that it is only one long series of law-suits; sixty years of official anarchy, and of conflicts in the executive, preceded and prepared the revolutionary state in which, for more than sixty years, France has been struggling. The reign of Louis XIV., which was so brilliant, but which sacrificed everything to itself, had put a stop to the political education of our country. " In establishing for himself," as a wise historian * has said, "a government, which he alone was capable of maintaining," the great monarch left to his successors a burden difficult to support. He had received from the hands of Henry IV. and Richelieu, a nation which was disengaged from the feudal chaos, and whose head, at least, was sufficiently ripe for new institutions; he offered to this nation every kind of glory; he contrived to make it accept and love, by surrounding it with the most seductive *prestige*, the most absolute power which had hitherto figured in our annals. He accomplished great and useful re-

* Droz, "History of the Reign of Louis XVI.," Introduction.

forms in all branches of the public administration; but, while he effected immense steps towards civilization, he did nothing to satisfy the wants which civilization brings with it, and which were to manifest themselves afterwards. He did nothing towards organising, in any form, a fundamental control of the chief power, a systematic intervention on the part of the country in its own destinies. After destroying the little that remained of earlier institutions, and concentrating the entire authority in himself, he said— " *l'Etat, c'est moi,*" and lived as if he was to be immortal, forgetting that a dictatorship is entirely personal, and disappears with the dictator. By the irresistible ascendancy of his glory, by the duration and brilliancy of a reign of seventy-two years, by the suppression of every hostile element, no monarch was ever placed in such a position as he to resolve that imperious problem, which is exhausting and consuming this age of confusion: the creation of institutions which will survive men. Unfortunately the tendency of unlimited power is not to limit itself, and history is still waiting for that miracle of an all-powerful sovereign, exercising his power towards his people like a father who is preparing his son to do without him.

Louis XIV. had scarcely descended into the grave when the dissolution of that government of which he was the soul, had already commenced. The three great social influences of that time—the nobility, the clergy, and the parliaments—who, if formed for political life by a firm hand, and invested with settled attributes, might have been able to direct the public mind, preside over the movement of the century, while at the same time moderating it, and avert the blind and violent irruption of the masses — these three great corporations, on issuing from a system in which they had only learned to obey in silence, were quite unfamiliar with the spirit of true government, and full of the most mean, annoying, and turbulent hostility. Their jealousies and their discords implanted that anarchy on the summit of society which was afterwards to descend into the inferior strata. "There are," wrote Montesquieu, at this period, "three kinds of estates, the church, the sword, and the gown; each one has a sovereign contempt for the two others." * Such, in fact, was the only link between the three classes which composed the French aristocracy. At one time we have the sword, triumphant at seeing the ambitious claims of the parliaments temporarily suspended by the *lits de justice;* and it must be seen with what superlative hatred and disdain the Duke de Saint-Simon celebrates this triumph. † At another, we

---

* "Lettres Persanes" (1721), forty-fourth letter.

† "It was then," he says, "that I enjoyed with a delight which cannot be expressed, the sight of those haughty jurists who would refuse all salvation to us, prostrate on their knees, and at our feet rendering homage to the throne, while we were seated with our hats

have the haughty Parliament, displaying its magnificence, and endeavouring to make every head succumb beneath the supremacy which it assumes.*   How-

on, by the side of this same throne. Our positions and their postures so entirely out of proportion to one another, in themselves, with the clearest evidence, plead the cause of those who truly and indeed are *laterales regis* against this *vas electum* of the *tiers état*. My eyes, fastened upon those proud *bourgeois*, ran over the long bench where they remained on their knees or standing up, and the ample folds of those furs, which undulated at each of the long and repeated genuflections . . . . . furs of a vile, dingy grey, painted to counterfeit ermine, and those heads uncovered and humbled, on a level with our feet.   During the registration I moved my eyes slowly around, and if I looked calmly at them, I could not resist the temptation of making up for it when I came to the chief president.   I overwhelmed him then at a hundred different times during the sitting, with a fixed, carefully prolonged stare.   Insult, contempt, disdain, triumph, were darted from my eyes into his very marrow ; frequently he lowered his glance when he caught my eye.   Once or twice he fixed his eyes on mine, and I took a pleasure in insulting him, by secret, but black smiles, which completed his confusion.   I revelled in his rage, and delighted in making him feel it."—Memoirs of the Duke de Saint-Simon, 8vo. ed., p. 140, vol. xvii., and following.

* The following shows how the Parliament of Toulouse treated a duke and peer of France, and Governor of Languedoc, who had executed the king's orders :—" The court in all its chambers assembled, considering that the Duke de Fitz-James, having reached the last extremity of audacity and madness, and forgetting his position as a subject, has dared to speak in the character of the sovereign to the members of the court, and to submit their liberty to insane conditions, &c., orders that the body of the said Duke de Fitz-James shall be taken and seized, in whatever part of the country he may be found; and that he shall be conducted and taken, in good and safe custody, into the prison of the con ever, this sullen inveterate struggle between the patrician order and the gown—this struggle, interrupted by temporary alliances against the arbitrary rule of ministers, is nothing compared to the fierce, permanent conflict between the Parliament and the Clergy; a conflict which was without result, for each of the contending parties assumed to be the supreme judge in the cause. Decrees were issued for arresting the curés who refused burial to the Jansenists; the parliaments were excommunicated by the bishops; priests thundered from the heights of the pulpit; the magistrates forced the priests by means of *huissiers,* to convey the sacraments where they directed; the Parliament of Paris sentenced to be burnt, on the same day, by the hands of the public executioner, Voltaire's "Philosophical Dictionary," and a Pastoral Letter from the Archbishop Christophe de Beaumont; all this mixed up with ridiculous controversies, of which the philosophers took advantage, in order to depreciate religion, forms the spectacle offered to us by the greater part of Louis XV.'s reign.

In the midst of all these quarrels, what became of the throne? Nominally absolute, in fact powerless, it acted without any further rule than the accident of

ciergerie of the court; and that in default of being apprehended, his goods shall be seized, &c." We need hardly say that the judgment was not acted upon, but the Duke de Fitz-James was recalled, although the king declared expressly that he had only obeyed his orders.

each day, and the momentary fortune of the combat. If it acted against the bishops, they closed the doors of the churches, and suspended the administration of the sacraments; if it wished to direct the parliaments, they suspended the course of justice, and visited society with a periodical paralysis. This embarrassment of the king is well represented in the following sketch, which we borrow from the Memoirs of Madame de Hausset:—"One day," she says, "the 'master' (Louis XV.) came in quite excited. I withdrew, but listened from my post. 'What is the matter?' said Madame, (Madame de Pompadour), to him. 'These men of the gown, and the clergy,' he replied, 'are always at daggers drawn; they drive me to despair with their quarrels; but I detest the great gowns much more than the others: my clergy is at bottom attached and faithful to me; the others would like to make me their ward.' 'Firmness,' said Madame, 'can alone bring them down.' ' Robert de Saint-Vincent is a firebrand, and I should like to exile him; but it would be a terrible job. On the other side, the archbishop has a head of iron, and is always seeking a pretext for a quarrel.' M. de Gontaut came in; the king was walking about in an excited state; suddenly he stopped and said, 'The regent was very wrong in allowing them the right to offer remonstrances; they will· finally be the destruction of the state.' 'Ah, Sire,' said M. de

Gontaut, 'it must be very strong for such little persons to be able to shake it!' 'You do not know what they do, and what they say,' replied the king; 'they are an assembly of republicans. That is enough about it, however; things will last as they are, during my time.'" *Things will last as they are during my time!* these words, even at that time, expressed the *nec plus ultra* of the French sovereign's ambition. At the present day a government lasting though a man's lifetime is a phenomenon with which we have ceased to be acquainted. For the rest, Louis XV. was not wrong in considering the opposition of the Parliaments as more dangerous than that of the clergy: in the indefinite character of its rights, and means of action, in the variety and obstinacy of its attacks, this opposition was, in the eighteenth century, the most active dissolving principle of the monarchy. It is generally known how things went on in Paris when the Parliament entered into a conflict with the royal power; the Parliament refused to register, a *lit de justice* interfered, Parliament persisted, its magistrates were exiled or imprisoned, concessions were made on each side, the opposition submitted or gained the victory, but the reconciliation of a day was soon followed by fresh disputes; such were the ordinary phases of the struggle in Paris. In the provinces, the conflict became still more grave and more difficult to settle.

The distance from the central power, the necessity of employing intermediaries, the contempt of each Parliament for everything that was not the royalty in person; and on the other hand, the brutality of the military agents, commissioned to enforce the king's will—all these circumstances led to scenes which demoralized the population. A remarkable and conscientious work, lately published,* enables us to appreciate this side, so little known, of the official anarchy of the eighteenth century. It shows us how the royalty endeavoured in vain to impose on the provincial Parliament the decisions of a section of a council of state, called the "grand council," a docile instrument of arbitrary power, by which it annulled their decisions; while the Parliaments refused to communicate with the *huissiers* of the grand council, who had been sent to supervise their registrations. Frequently a *huissier* of the grand council, and a *huissier* from the Parliament of the province, arrived to convey to the inhabitants of the same commune, two orders which were diametrically opposite, and whichever one of the two *huissiers* had *gendarmes* at his service, arrested the other. At another period, the king's commissary arrives in

* "History of the Parliament of Normandy," by M. Floquet. It would be very desirable for each of the twelve parliaments of France, under the ancient *régime*, to be the subject of an equally valuable work.

the shape of a general, with troops to enforce the
submission of the Parliaments. The magistrates
receive him on their seats, and refuse to give up their
registers.   Dragoon officers take the register by
force, and, pen in hand, strike out the decisions of
justice.   The magistrates draw up an accusation
against the executants of the king's orders, and
cause their judgment to be proclaimed on the very
steps of the court, before an excited crowd.   The
governor of the province would then cause all the
presses to be seized, in order to prevent the publication of the magistrates' decision. The Procureur-
General called upon, at the same time, by the two
conflicting authorities, to transmit to all the sub-
ordinate judges, two contradictory decisions, and
not daring to offer resistance to either, made it his
duty to promulgate at the same time, the affirmative and the negative.   The Parliament suspended
the administration of justice during four months,
until the king admitted its remonstrances.   All the
other Parliaments took the part of the one which
resisted.   The irritated king summoned the magistrates to Versailles, reprimanded them, exiled them,
and always ended by yielding and revoking his
own acts in the most imperative manner, while the
magistrates, who always gained the victory with the
forms of respect, took their places again amid the applause of the multitude, illuminations, *feux de joie,*

te deums, and deputations from all the provinces, which came to congratulate them on their energy.

Such was the pernicious system of conflicts in the executive, under which our fathers were brought up. Thus did France prepare herself, little by little, for entering upon her revolutionary career; thus seeing every day, in all parts of the country, the church at war with the magistracy, the magistracy at war with the throne, the people contracted more and more a contempt for authority, and consequently an idolatry for mere force. Certainly Parliaments such as they had been constituted since the time of Philippe le Bel, with functions of an essentially judicial character, would have been puzzled to say from whom they held the mission they assumed of representing the national will, and controlling the acts of the sovereign. "One of the most enlightened and zealous parliamentarians," says Duclos, "whom I asked to point out in a precise manner the limits which separated the usurpation from the rights of Parliaments, replied to me: 'The principles of this question are very obscure; but, as regards the fact, a Parliament is strong under a weak king, and weak under a strong one. A minister acting in good faith,' adds Duclos, 'would, perhaps, give the same answer if he were obliged to explain himself on the subject of the king's power relatively to the nation.'" The rights of the Parliaments, then, were doubtful, but those of the throne were not less so; on the land of France, *autocracy*, pure and simple, may have been accepted or undergone sometimes as a fact: it has never been recognised as a right. "It is liberty," says Madame de Staël, "that is ancient, and despotism that is modern." * Fatigued by the sanguinary convulsions of the seventeenth century, and the troubles of the Fronde, the nation had bowed with docility beneath the glorious sceptre of Louis XIV.; this sceptre, fallen into the hands of Louis XV., no longer inspired respect; the claim of a king, who was governed by depraved women and contemptible favourites, to dispose of it at will and render account of his actions to God alone, humiliated and irritated it. The spirit of resistance to arbitrary power was the general spirit; in the absence of all other guarantee, the Parliaments presented themselves as the sole barrier which could be opposed to the caprices of an unbridled power; and, whatever were the particular vices of these amphibious bodies, which were at once judicial and political, in spite of their prejudices, their fanaticism in favour of the existing state of things and their systematic repugnance to all reforms, even the most just and wise, whenever they made head against the wishes of the king, they had the public opinion in their favour.

---

* "Considérations sur la Révolution Française," p. 25.

Supported by this opinion, the Parliaments found their ascendancy increasing every day; linked closely together, they declared themselves "the members of one sole and indivisible body, inherent to the monarchy, the organ of the nation, and the essential depository of its liberty, its interests, and its rights," and each of their combats with the king used to terminate in victory, when an individual issuing from their own body, the chancellor Maupeou, a man of audacious and obstinate disposition, undertook either to subject or destroy them.

Supported by Madame du Barry, who governed the king, and who was animated by the resentment of the Duke d'Aiguillon, branded as he had been by a judgment of the Parliament of Paris, the chancellor Maupeou extorted from the hesitation of Louis XV. the edict of December 7, 1770, which changed the whole organisation of the Parliaments; the Parliament of Paris protested against and rejected the edict. The chancellor, instead of following the ordinary course, broke up the Parliament of Paris, confiscated the appointments of the magistrates, exiled them, and formed a new Parliament, composed for the greater part of members of the grand council. The eleven provincial Parliaments addressed the most vehement remonstrances to the king; that of Normandy went so far as to issue a judgment, which declared the new magistrates to be "usurpers, perjurers, and traitors," and all acts emanating from this " bastard tribunal " to be null. All the princes of the blood, with the exception of one only, refused to recognise the judges appointed by Maupeou; and thirteen peers adhered to this protest. The Cour des Aides also protested, through the eloquent voice of Malesherbes. The chancellor resisted the storm; by his means admission to court was refused to all the dissentient princes. He broke up the Cour des Aides, dissolved successively all the provincial Parliaments, and re-formed them in the midst of an unheard of excitement. " This is not a man," writes Madame du Deffand, " it is a devil; everything here is in a state of subversion, of which it is impossible to see the end; it is chaos—it is the end of the world." To break up these ancient and formidable bodies, the existence of which seemed inseparable from the monarchy, and the suppression of which placed France beneath a government similar to that of Turkey or Russia, was indeed an enterprise of the most hazardous kind. The chancellor had taken care to soften it down and colour it, by joining to it some important reforms which had long been called for by all right-minded persons: such as the abolition of the sale-ability of government places; the substitution of fixed salaries for the fees which, according to the old custom used to be paid to the judges by the litigants, so as to assure the gratuitous administration of justice; the establishment of superior courts in larger numbers, and the diminution of the number of petty courts, so as to lessen the distance between the plaintiffs and defendants on the one side, and the tribunals who had to decide finally upon their cases on the other. Doubtless these measures, combined with the animosity he retained for the old Parliaments, determined Voltaire to side with the chancellor, but he was not followed in this movement; and if the mass of the people, already prepared by the obstinate disputes of which we have just given a picture to submit to a *coup* executed with resolution, did not quite understand all the importance of Maupeou's enterprise, and at first exhibited some indifference regarding it—all the enlightened classes of society refused to purchase a few useful reforms at the price of an ignominious servitude, and declared with energy in favour of the abolished magistracy. The public anger was soon let loose, and all kinds of sarcasms and pamphlets* were directed against the king, his mistress, the chancellor and the new Parliament. The latter, which had been formed hastily out of heterogeneous elements, and in which many men of little repute had been introduced, found at the beginning neither barristers nor solicitors, nor suitors willing to appear before it. Maupeou,

* In Bachaumont the greater part of these innumerable pamphlets in prose or verse, are reproduced.

however, counting on the changeable nature of the French, met the public clamour with much perseverance; at the expiration of a year the greater number of the advocates were tired of being silent; under the influence of the celebrated Gerbier, and the same Caillard whose violence towards Beaumarchais we have already witnessed, re-assumed their functions. *
The dissentient princes begged to be restored to favour; the magistrates who had been dismissed consented to a compromise for the loss of their appointments; the number of pamphlets diminished; things returned to their ordinary course, everything seemed to have been made calm; Maupeou considered his triumph assured, and boasted of having rescued the crown from the gown; he was deceived. When all the intelligent and honest portion of a nation feels its dignity wounded, the wound may close in appearance, but it does not heal. That which has in the first instance been a flame, becomes a latent fire, which smoulders under the ash, and which the least spark is

---

* It was upon this subject that the following vaudeville was circulated:—

> L'honneur des avocàts,
> Jadis si délicats,
> N'est plus qu'une fumée;
> Leur troup diffamée
> Subit le joug enfin,
> Et de Caillard avide
> La prudence décide
> Qu'il vaut bien mieux mourir de honte que de faim.

sufficient to revive. It was reserved for Beaumarchais to revive, with an action about fifteen louis, the flame which was to devour Maupeou and his Parliament.

It will be remembered what the situation of the author of " The Barber of Seville " was in April 1773, when his action against the Count de La Blache was under the consideration of the court of appeal. Imprisoned at For-l'Evêque, he had obtained, as the period forgiving judgment drew near, permission to go out during the day to have interviews with his judges, according to the custom of the period. The affair had been deliberated upon, and was to be decided from the report of a councillor named Goëzman. This Goëzman, who was first a councillor at the Supreme Council of Alsace, had sold his appointment, and in 1765 had come to Paris, where he established himself. He was a jurisconsult of some learning; among other works he had published a " Treatise on the Common Law of Fiefs," which was not without merit. But to judge of him by various particulars which I find among Beaumarchais' papers, whether the value of his appointment in Alsace did not belong to him, or whether it had been dissipated by him, it would appear that the life he led in Paris was to some extent that of an adventurer, and rather questionable as regarded its morality, when the Maupeou chancellor introduced him in 1771 into the ill-received body which he had just established in place of the old Parliament.

This judge had married, for his second wife, a woman who was still young and sufficiently pretty, and whose conversation was calculated to do little honour to her husband's honesty and her own, for it was proved, in the course of the law-suit, of which we are about to give an account, that she had said before witnesses, " It would be impossible to live decently with what we get, but we know the art of plucking the fowl without making it cry out."   It can be seen that if the chancellor Maupeou suppressed the gratuities, some of the new magistrates possessed the secret of replacing them with advantage.   Remarks of the above nature were frequently made by Madame Goëzman at the house of a librarian named Lejay, who sold the works of the husband, and received the visits of the wife.   This librarian, who did not know Beaumarchais, hearing from a mutual friend that he was in despair at not being able to gain access to the reporter, informed him that the only means of obtaining audiences from, and insuring the equity of the judge who had to prepare the report, was by making a present to his wife, and he accordingly asked for 200 louis to give her. Beaumarchais gave 100 louis, and a watch adorned with diamonds of equal value ; Madame Goëzman wanted fifteen louis more, which she said were for her husband's secretary. The fifteen louis were sent ; the lady declared to Lejay, that if Beaumarchais lost his action, all he gave would be restored to him, except .

the fifteen louis, which in any case would remain the property of the secretary. The day afterwards, Beaumarchais obtained an audience from the reporter Goëzman; two days after that, this judge decided against him. Madame Goëzman returned faithfully the hundred louis and the watch; but Beaumarchais having inquired of the secretary, to whom in the course of the trial he had already given ten louis, whether he had received in addition fifteen louis from Madame Goëzman, ascertained that she had given nothing to him, and that the fifteen louis had remained in her pocket. Irritated already by the loss of an action which was equally important to his fortune and his honour, he disapproved of Madame Goëzman indulging in so dishonest a speculation, and decided to write to her and claim the fifteen louis. This was a grave step; for if the councillor's wife refused to restore the money and denied having received it, if Beaumarchais insisted upon having it, and if the affair made a noise, a very dangerous quarrel might arise out of it. But the step with its dangers also presented its advantages: persuaded, with or without reason, that the Count de La Blache had given more money than himself to the councillor Goëzman, Beaumarchais in meeting the danger of a personal dispute with this magistrate, hoped to convict him of venality, and thus with greater ease get the judgment which had been made upon his report annulled.

What he had foreseen took place : Madame Goëzman, obliged either to admit the misappropriation of the fifteen louis, and restore them, or to deny that she had received them, took the latter course. She declared loudly that presents had been offered to her by Beaumarchais, with a view of gaining her husband's interest; but that she had refused his criminal offer. Goëzman interfered, and denounced Beaumarchais to the Parliament as guilty of having calumniated the wife of a judge, after having vainly endeavoured to corrupt her, and through her to corrupt her husband.

As the fact of the presents having been accepted and kept until after the decision of the La Blache suit, and of the fifteen louis having been asked for and retained by Madame Goëzman, was proved in the clearest manner by judicial investigation, it is difficult to understand how the husband of this lady had the imprudence to institute such an action. It may be supposed that, in the first instance, he was ignorant of the shameful traffic which his wife had been pursuing; it may be supposed that the latter, when she took the 100 louis and the watch, and still required fifteen louis more, had said to herself : " I shall not speak about the matter to my husband; if he decides in favour of Beaumarchais and makes him gain his action, the latter, delighted with the result, will keep the secret, I shall retain the whole, and my husband, who otherwise is ignorant of what has taken place between us, will not be compromised. If, on the other hand, my husband is unfavourable to Beaumarchais, and he loses his action, I will restore him the 100 louis and the watch; as it is agreed that the fifteen louis, which I have said were destined for my husband's secretary, cannot be claimed back, even in case of the action being lost, I will keep them for myself, so that in any case there will be a slight profit.   Even if Beaumarchais should happen to hear that these fifteen louis had not been disposed of in the manner stated, he would not dare to claim the return of such a petty sum, which in any case was to cease to be his, and to expose himself to a grave accusation; if he dared to do so, I would tell my husband that he had tried to corrupt me, and that I had repelled his offers of bribery, as would be proved by my having sent back the 100 louis and the watch; that, as for the fifteen louis which he claims, it is a mere fable, which he has invented in revenge for not having succeeded in bribing me; and as it is scarcely natural that the wife of a councillor of the Parliament, who sends back 100 louis, and a watch of the same value, would persist in keeping fifteen louis,* my husband will not doubt my veracity, and will have Beaumarchais punished."

---

* The improbability of this is in fact one of the principal arguments which Madame Goëzman used in her defence. But, she had begun by concealing the fact that she had kept the hundred louis two days, and had only restored them after the decision of the action; and when the

Such a train of reasoning as this would be nothing
astonishing in the case of a woman who was as
thoughtless as she was rapacious and vulgar; but it
is far less probable that the councillor, Goëzman, a
man who had seen life, and who was an experienced
criminal lawyer, could have been deceived by his
wife's reasoning, and that upon her simple affirma-
tion, he could have been led to believe that Beaumarchais was mad enough to lay himself open to an inevi-
table condemnation, by daring to claim fifteen louis,
which had *not* been received, and kept by Madame
Goëzman. It appears to me, beyond doubt then, that
directly he heard of Beaumarchais' claim, Goëzman,
by interrogating the different persons who had been
mixed up with all this huckstering, must have convinced himself that his wife had compromised herself in a grave manner. Once compromised however by her, he had to choose between certain
courses of action, all of which, in the case of a
discontented and indiscreet suitor, appeared likely
to damage his reputation: the one on which he
ultimately determined was incontestably the boldest,
but also the most unjust of all. Starting from the
idea that Beaumarchais was not powerful enough to

retractation of the bookseller Lejay, who in the first instance stated a
falsehood, at the instigation of her husband, obliged her to confess
this fact, she declared that Lejay left the 100 louis, without her
knowledge, in a flower-case, which stood on the mantelpiece. It need
not be said that Lejay refuted her on this point, as on all the others.

resist him, he imagined, that by taking the initiative in the contest, and manœuvring so as tò prevent the truth from becoming apparent, he could at the same time ruin the person who had given the fifteen louis, and save the one who after asking for them to give to another, had appropriated them to her own benefit. It will be seen directly, how Goëzman's plans were disconcerted and how severely they were punished.

What confirms me in my opinion, that this magistrate acted in bad faith, from the moment of the accusation, is not only the result of the action, after which he received the condemnation of his colleagues, and was obliged to quit his office—for they might only have wished to visit the faults of his wife on his own want of skill; but in the papers, subsequently given up to Beaumarchais by M. de Sartines, I find it proved that before having recourse to the Parliament, Goëzman tried to get rid of this importunate suitor, by means of a *lettre de cachet*, and that for an instant he really hoped this trifling service would be rendered to him, for, on the 5th June, 1773, he wrote to M. de Sartines the following note : —

"I beg that *the punishment* may appear to proceed, in a *sufficiently evident manner*, from the insult offered to my wife, and indirectly to myself. Will you be kind enough to inform me, to-morrow, what course has been adopted, and rely on my eternal devotion."

As the government did not dare to risk such an injustice, and as the story of the fifteen louis was beginning to be spread about, even in the Palais-de-Justice itself, the councillor Goëzman took precautions to render the attack irresistible. He summoned the bookseller, Lejay, who had been his wife's agent, and, after frightening him by threats, and reassuring him at the same time as to the consequences of the deed he required from him, made him copy the minute of a false affidavit, which he had prepared himself, and in which Lejay, corroborating the falsehoods of Madame Goëzman, declared that Beaumarchais had urged him to endeavour to corrupt this lady, by making her offers of presents, but that she had indignantly rejected them all. Armed with this false affidavit, he decided at last to call down the vengeance of the Parliament on the head of a man who had been much calumniated, and over whom he expected to gain an easy triumph.

Beaumarchais' disrepute was, indeed, at its height. The judgment given in the La Blache suit, in accordance with the report of this same Goëzman, had cast a stain on his honour, and destroyed his fortune. His victorious adversary had seized all his goods, and did not leave him a moment's repose. In the midst of this distress, he found himself charged by a judge with bribery and calumny, before other judges who were interested in finding him guilty.

This new prosecution, being of a criminal nature, had, according to the laws of the period, to be conducted secretly, and decided with closed doors. The Maupeou Parliament could not do otherwise than hasten to punish, with the most extreme rigour, a prisoner who was brought before it charged with actions which endangered the dignity and the very existence of this judicial body, already the object of so much hatred; and criminal jurisprudence was then allowed a frightful latitude, for, in the case of a person charged with the offence in question, it permitted the most severe punishment, after the punishment of death, *omnia citra mortem.*

Beaumarchais, then, had reached that extreme point, in reference to which the poet has said, *Una salus victis nullam sperare salutem.* Placed between two chances—which were about equal—that of being sacrificed if he defended himself in the regular manner before his judges, and that of obtaining, at least, some attention, if he succeeded in raising public opinion in his favour, he did not hesitate. While the most clear-sighted had still doubts about that growing power, opinion, Beaumarchais had no doubts at all, and trusted to it boldly. No advocate dared to take his part against so redoubtable an adversary as Goëzman; he determined to be his own advocate, to plead his own cause, and he will be seen to plead it before all the world. He will trample under foot the regulations which order criminal prosecutions to be kept secret, which prevent the judges from being judged by the nation, and while preparations are being made for stifling him in the dark, he will introduce light everywhere, and will summon opinion to his aid ; but in order that public opinion may reply to the appeal of a man who is unknown, or only known unfavourably, it is necessary that this man should be able to attract readers, retain them, excite their passion, their indignation, their pity, and at the same time amuse them. The state of things was such, that Beaumarchais was obliged, we may almost say under pain of death, to display a marvellous talent, in giving to an affair, which was of little interest in itself, all the interest of a drama, a comedy, and a romance. If he contents himself with discussing the question in a becoming manner, if he confines himself to the facts of his case, if he cannot contrive to connect with this case attractive social details, and important political questions, if he is not at the same time very pathetic and very humorous; if, in a word, he does not have a popular success he is lost : the new Parliament will be the more unmerciful towards him, inasmuch as he has shown himself mistrustful of the justice with closed doors of the new Parliament; and he has in perspective—*omnia citra mortem.*

Such an alternative, calculated as it was to paralyse an ordinary mind, was precisely the goad which

...is on, and gave him a kind of fever, ...ived in the rapid and continuous ...style, even in the argumentative

...of view, his case was not so simple ...Harpe, and other writers who like ...ry lightly over the ground-work ...repel the accusation of calumny, ...rove that he had given money to ...and, in this case, how was he to ...of bribery? By endeavouring ...did not wish to purchase the ...d when he gave money to the ...nly wished to obtain those au- ...indispensable, which he could ...m the justice of the councillor, ...vife chose to set a pecuniary ...e, at the commencement of the ...nced that his wife would not ...eavoured, on his side, to prove ...; accordingly, he did not fail ...a, that it was scarcely probable ...eady heard, after the pleadings, ...cision would have offered to ...rter 100 louis, a watch of ...5 louis; that is to say, more ...ely to obtain the privilege of ...ions to this reporter who was

G

impartial. Beaumarchais replied, that he had of
nothing; that it had all been asked for; that
only question between him and Madame Goë
had been with regard to audiences, and that
law dealt with facts, and not with probabil
Then, turning the weapon of probability with d
skill against the accuser himself, he showed th
was the accomplice of his wife, that he was
open to the suspicion of having sold his justi
the highest bidder, and that he was now endea
ing to reduce to silence and to annihilate the s
whom he had already sacrificed. Beaumarchai
tention in paying Madame Goëzman might
appeared equivocal; nevertheless, one thing whic
sulted clearly from the debate was, that if ther
been any idea of corruption, the thought had
ceeded not from Beaumarchais, but from the (
man family; that Beaumarchais, who knew n
the wife of the judge nor the bookseller who
spoken in her name, had only submitted to the
ditions imposed upon him. And when the a
breaking through all the artifices of his accuse
forcing the witnesses who had been suborned
to retract or remain silent, and those who had
intimidated to speak, succeeded in bringing a
ignoble and odious side of the affair to light,
it was clearly shown that the wife of a councill
longing to the new Parliament had basely mis

priated a miserable sum of fifteen louis, and that the husband, in order to conceal the misappropriation, was pursuing to death the suitor who had asked to have his fifteen louis returned, the indignation of the public against Goëzman knew no bounds; they refused to look upon him as what he really, I think, was in this affair— a magistrate involved first of all by his wife, without being aware of it, in an awkward matter, and who afterwards endeavoured to get out of it *per fas et nefas;* they refused to admit that he was a stranger to the sordid action, which Beaumarchais, encouraged by the public, did not fear to speak of before the assembled Parliament as an act of swindling, and took a pleasure in covering the councillor Goëzman and the detested body to which he belonged with the same contempt, and the same accusations of dishonesty, venality and injustice. This last was the dangerous point of the discussion; in touching upon it with a talent which exhibited equal audacity and prudence, by means of the most transparent allusions and the most deadly reticence, this Beaumarchais, so decried the day before, became suddenly the favoured organ of the public anger, and the minister of the public vengeance in connexion with the *coup d'état* which had destroyed the old magistracy.

To the political interest of this action was joined the interest mingled with surprise, which was excited by a man whose previous works had appeared mediocre, exhibiting the most original, the most varied talent, and giving to his judicial pleadings every kind of literary beauty and ornament. Enough has been said in regard to the literary merits of the Memorials against Goëzman, and we have no intention of dwelling on a worn-out subject. We shall only endeavour to study those celebrated polemics under their least-known aspect.

On reading the pleadings of Beaumarchais now, we are sometimes shocked by the excessive and insulting nature of his irony and invective. An eminent critic, who is an exquisite appreciator of the good and the beautiful, M. Villemain, admires the animated and versatile eloquence of these brilliant productions, but cannot help exclaiming against certain portions, which he says shock our ideas of decency and truth.* His contemporaries were, however, much less struck than ourselves with the violence of his language, which proceeded from two causes—the one general, the other particular.

At this period, the press was not regulated, and indeed was scarcely tolerated by law; but it was active in spite of legislation, under the influence of a social necessity which is more powerful than legislation, and, as a natural consequence, went beyond bounds. In looking over the licentious

* Française Cours de Littérature—Tableau du XVIIIᵉ siècle, IIIᵉ parte, 9ᵉ leçon.

and unscrupulous works of every kind, which circulated everywhere during the period we speak of, one would scarcely suspect that people were then living, as regarded the press, beneath the effect of a certain edict of 1769, which admitted no compromise, since it condemned simply *to death every author of writings tending to excite the public mind.* It was concluded from this, that dull and tedious writers were alone certain not to be hanged, and every one wrote without paying more attention to the edict than if it had never existed. Laws, as has been said with reason, which are in open contradiction with the ideas and manners of a people, are soon looked upon by it as words, and as words only.

The same silent system which it was vainly endeavoured to apply to public affairs, was not less vainly attempted in the matter of judicial proceedings. The law courts assumed to surround themselves with mystery, like the government, and at no epoch did more scandalous law-suits produce more offensive and venomous libels. In the present day, when the system of publicity is gaining more and more extension—in the present day, when it is in general, and with the exception of accidental restrictions, sanctioned by laws which regulate without stifling it, through constant use—it gets to be used with moderation, and finds a salutary and permanent control in public

opinion. When the doors of the tribunals are open
to all, when every plaintiff and every defendant can
say or cause to be said publicly by his advocate,
whatever is important to his case; and when there are
journals to print the reports, the personal statements
which were exchanged between exasperated suitors,
have no longer any meaning: they are looked upon
as things apart, and if a few sometimes appear,
they always exhibit a certain reserve. All polemic
writings, on the contrary, which were published in
the eighteenth century, acquired from the very fact of
their illegality an indecorousness and violence of style,
which produced no astonishment, and seemed almost
excused by the prohibition itself.

Another cause which made the public look upon
Beaumarchais' incisive style with great indulgence
was, that if he was sometimes violent, his adversaries, whose now forgotten Memorials were read at
the same time as his own, were remarkable for a
violence which was even greater. He was happy
enough to have only to fight against enemies who,
besides being very ridiculous, were also very much
enraged and very malicious, in intention at all events.
"People laughed," says La Harpe, with justice, "to
see them scarified; for they had daggers in their
hands."

CHAPTER XII.

THE Memorials of Beaumarchais' antagonists have
become very rare. I procured them in order to get at
the true aspect of this contest. In reading them, we
perceive more clearly to how great a degree the man
they were prosecuting possessed the genius of observation, with how much penetration he discerned, with
what justness he reproduced the exact shade of platitude, cunning, or malice, which distinguished each of
his enemies. It is seen, also, that, taken altogether,
the moderation was on his side; that he did not begin
to make desperate attacks, until he had been himself
attacked beyond bounds and without shame. Thus,
in his first Memorial he contents himself with expos-
ing the facts clearly and precisely; he discusses the
question of right; repels the accusation of Goëzman,
but is very reserved in his language, and very chary
of personalities. Hardly had he published his Me-

morial, than five furious adversaries rushed almost simultaneously upon him. It was not till then that he crossed swords, and took the offensive with a vigour which went on increasing until he had stretched on the ground the five champions, whom we are about to pass hastily in review.

The first who appears is Madame Goëzman, who writes under her husband's dictation, and throws at Beaumarchais' head a quarto of seventy-four pages, bristling with law terms and Latin quotations. Nothing can be more heavy or more anomalous than this language uttered by a lawyer who assumes the mask of a woman, and says "I have taken in all the facts of this case, as *far as it is in the power of a woman to do so*;" or, "his recrimination must then be rejected, conformably to that law *which I have heard cited, neganda est accusatis, licentia criminandi.*" Beaumarchais sums up the profound stupidity of this document very wittily, when he exclaims, "An ingenuous woman is announced to me, and I am introduced to a German publicist." But if the Memorial is ridiculous in form, it is in substance extremely violent. "My mind" — it is thus that Madame Goëzman commences—"has been divided between astonishment, surprise, and horror, in reading the libel which M. Caron has just spread abroad. The audacity of the author astonishes, the number and atrocity of his impostures excite surprise, the idea he gives of himself produces horror." When it is reflected that the honest lady who speaks thus has in her drawer the fifteen louis, the claiming of which excites her surprise, her astonishment, and her horror, one is inclined to excuse Beaumarchais for having indulged in some freedoms of speech in reference to her. It is well known, however, with what a mixture of ironical politeness and clenching argument he refutes, irritates, embarrasses, compliments, and confounds Madame Goëzman. Who has not burst into a laugh on reading the excellent comedy scene, in which he represents himself conversing with her before the registrar? The scene is so amusing, that one is inclined to take it for an imaginary sketch; it is nothing of the kind, however. The second Memorial, in which Madame Goëzman replies to Beaumarchais' statement, answers completely to the idea he gives us of her. Here we have no longer the husband speaking, but the lady herself. The tone is quite that of a woman in a passion: " I reproached M. Caron," she says, "when I met him, with being an *atrocious* man, and known to be such. The epithet appears to have offended him, I must therefore justify it." She divides her Memorial into *first, second, third atrocity*, and after this beautiful division concludes in these words: " That was not sufficient for you, atrocious man; you dared in the presence of the commissary, the registrar, and another person, to propose that I should go over to your side, to endeavour to render my husband odious in my sight. Your audacity extended even further, you dared to add. (why am I obliged to recal speeches as insolent as they are humiliating to me?)—you dared to add, I say, that you would at last make me hear you; that your attentions would one day be not displeasing to me; that . . . . I dare not finish—I dare not call you what you are!"

This display of feminine vanity in so important an affair gives a notion of Madame Goëzman's strength of character.   The amusing reply of Beaumarchais, when wishing to reassure the alarmed modesty of his fair enemy, is known.   In defending himself from the charge of having made, in presence of an austere registrar, pen in hand, observations of a nature that could only be indicated by dots, he reminded her, that if in the first instance she called him an atrocious man, she only considered him *bien malin*, after he had addressed her in the following terms:—"I call upon you, Madame, to tell us instantly, without reflection and without preparation, why you state in all your interrogatories that you are thirty, when your countenance contradicts you, and shows that you are only eighteen." The judge, Goëzman, the accuser, who conducted the whole affair, did not make his appearance personally until the middle of the suit; he had reckoned upon a rapid and easy triumph; but the dispute became complicated by the introduction of facts, which told very much against him. Beaumarchais, driven to extremities by the insinuation of poisoning, and the accusation of forgery, which the magistrate ventured to make in his wife's Memorials, took reprisals, and examined in his turn the life of Goëzman. After proving that, in the pending law-suit, he had induced the bookseller, Lejay, to make a false affidavit, he discovered that some time previously, in order to conceal certain immoral conduct, Goëzman had signed a certificate of baptism under a false name, and denounced him, in his turn, before the Parliament as a forger. A public cry was raised against him, the Maupeou Parliament was obliged to decree the personal suspension of one of its members, and a councillor of the grand chamber was seen to combine the position of accuser with that of accused. The opening of his Memorial gives a very precise idea of the situation. " A cry has been raised," he says, " and an unfortunate combination of circumstances, together with the malicious pleasure of inculpating a magistrate at the present juncture, have instantly caused an infinity of echoes. The belief has spread like a secret contagion; a storm has been formed, which has settled above my head," &c. If Goëzman continued to speak in this style he might inspire some interest; but, soon afterwards, he is seen getting into a passion, and exhibits equal anger and bad.

faith towards a man who had only defended himself from his attacks. At this period of the suit, the councillor, even if we adopt the utterly improbable supposition that he had hitherto been deceived by his wife, could no longer doubt that the latter had asked for, received, and kept the fifteen louis. He must also have known very well that Beaumarchais had employed no corrupt artifice for transmitting them to her, other than that of accepting the intervention of an agent, who was representing her, and with whom she alone was acquainted; in spite of all this, he persisted more than ever in blackening his adversary's reputation, and, nevertheless, as he felt that his accusation (the venality of his wife once established) gave him an odious part to sustain, he concluded with false protéstations of kindness, which his whole conduct disproved, and which only showed that he was conscious of being compromised.

The influence of Beaumarchais' Memorials is seen even in the pleadings of Goëzman. Following the example of Beaumarchais, whom he had reproached so much with unveiling to the public the mysteries of the tribunal, the councillor in his own turn violated the established rules. We know how Beaumarchais excels in representing two suitors, pleading alternately before a magistrate, and examining one another face to facc. Goëzman now represents himself examining Beaumarchais: " I called upon him," he says, "to declare why, on the following day, he made my wife the offer of a valuable jewel—he wandered from the question. Called upon to state why he made use of the word '*traiter*' in the letter he wrote to my wife—he wandered from the question." And thus, with the words "wandered from the question," Goëzman ingeniously replaces his antagonist's replies. The process was convenient, and involved very little trouble ; but the public took the liberty of doubting whether Beaumarchais wandered away from the question so readily, and laughed at Goëzman while they were waiting for Beaumarchais to publish his account of the confrontation. This confrontation was to form the subject of a sixth* Memorial, which was not drawn up—the decision, which was given soon afterwards, rendering it useless ; but we may conjecture that it would have been very comic, from Goëzman's own Memorial, for when he has to represent Beaumarchais examining him in his turn, the magistrate declines to go any further, "that he may not have to reproduce a revolting exhibition of audacity, and insolence ;" he gives us, however, an excellent idea of it in the following little sketch : " He showed me, as he placed his two hands

---

* Generally speaking, only four of Beaumarchais' Memorials, in connection with the Goëzman affair, are known ; but there are five, including the supplement to the first, which, after the fourth, is the most interesting of all. .

together, a considerable hollow space between them, which, he said, he could fill with the journals he had procured clandestinely that referred to my conduct, since my existence had become a matter of interest to him. I contented myself with telling him, in a laughing manner, that, in a country where the Inquisition existed, I was sure he would have made an excellent familiar; and that it was astonishing the Holy office had not retained him in Spain, where he had made such a glorious journey; but that, in France, where, to act as a spy on citizens, is a public crime, his little trade might take him, some day, a few hundred leagues away from Paris, in the direction of the coast." The judge's answer is not badly turned; but it is not, perhaps, very magisterial, and appears to come from a man to whom the word " Inquisition" inspires some dread.

The other three adversaries of Beaumarchais are not less useful to him than the first; one is a kind of speculative banker, named Bertrand, who had, first of all, acted on his behalf, and had treated in his name with Madame Goëzman's friend the bookseller. Alarmed at the accusation made by the councillor, and fearing to encounter his hatred, Bertrand, after in the first instance giving the true particulars, seemed disposed to take what appeared the stronger side, and was inclined to attack Beaumarchais, for the benefit of Madame Goëzman. The first of Beaumarchais' Memorials took him up mildly and politely enough. Bertrand, whose fear rendered him very irritable against the accused, replied in an insulting paper, which bore this epigraph from the Psalms: "*Judica me, Deus, et discerne causam meam de gente non sanctâ, et ab homine iniquo et doloso erue me.*" Beaumarchais could only take his revenge on the "great Bertrand," by inflicting on him the celebrity of ridicule. Here, as everywhere, the shades of character are perfectly rendered. In vain does Bertrand attempt to deal blows of terrific force; in vain does he compose phrases in the style of the following: "A cynical rhetorician—a buffoon, an unblushing sophist, a deceptive painter, who finds in his own soul the filth with which he tarnishes the garment of innocence, malevolent from necessity and from taste, his hard, vindictive, implacable heart—becomes dizzy from its passing triumph, and stifles feeling humanity without remorse." Instead of returning rage for rage, Beaumarchais contented himself with giving Bertrand's portrait: he depicts him as a chatterer, greedy of gain, vacillating, and at once timid and passionate, but more foolish even than malicious, such, in a word, as he exhibits himself in the four grotesque Memorials, with which he has enriched this famous law-suit.

The fourth champion who rushes headlong at Beaumarchais, and is transfixed at the first thrust, is a romance writer of the time, who was rather amusing in the funereal style, and who prided himself on having, to use his own words, "the rotundity of sentiment."* This was d'Arnaud-Baculard, who, to make himself agreeable to Goëzman, wrote a letter, containing a false piece of information, and who, after being very politely corrected in the first Memorial of Beaumarchais, replied as follows : " Yes, I was on foot, and in the Rue de Condé I met M. Caron in his carriage, *in his carriage !*" And as Beaumarchais had said that d'Arnaud had a sombre expression, d'Arnaud became indignant, and exclaimed, " I had not a sombre expression, but I was deeply impressed : a sombre expression only becomes those persons who are *ruminating crime*, who are labouring to stifle remorse, and to do fresh injury. . . . Such persons may be followed step by step in their countenances ; they are marching towards the eruption. . . . There are hearts in which I shudder to read ; I measure within them all the *sombre depths of hell.* At such a time I exclaim : ' Thou sleepest, Jupiter ! Of what use, then, are thy thunderbolts ? ' "

It is seen that if d'Arnaud in his turn does no harm, it is not for want of good will. It will, perhaps, be interesting to reproduce here the answer of Beaumarchais ; it will be seen with what justice he gives every

* *L'embonpoint du sentiment.*

one what he deserves, and what a charming serenity he displays in the contest. He commences by reproducing d'Arnaud's phrase in reference to the carriage :—

" ' In his carriage,' you repeat, with a large note of admiration. Would not any one think, after the sad ' Yes, I was on foot,' and the large note of admiration which runs after my carriage, that you were the very personification of envy ; but I, who know you to be a good sort of man, am aware, that your phrase, ' in his carriage,' does not mean that you were sorry to see me in my carriage, but only sorry that I did not see you in yours.

"But console yourself, Sir ; the carriage in which I was riding had already ceased to belong to me when you saw me in it. The Count de La Blache had had it seized with all the rest of my property : men, entitled *à hautes armes*, with blue coats, cartouche belts, and muskets of menacing aspect, were keeping their eyes on it at my house, together with the whole of my furniture ; and, in order to cause you, in spite of myself, the mortification of seeing me *in my carriage*, I had been obliged, the same day, to undergo that of soliciting from the *huissiers*, with my hat in one hand and a crown-piece in the other, permission to make use of it, which, if you will allow me to say so, I did every morning; and whilst I am now speaking to you with so much tranquillity the same distress still exists in my house.

"How unjust people are ! They envy and hate a man whom they think happy, and who would frequently give something to be in the place of the pedestrian who detests him on account of his carriage. Myself, for example—can anything be more calculated than my present situation to throw me into a state of despair ? But I am something like the cousin of Heloise : I may weep as much as I like, a laugh is sure to escape on one side or the other. That is what renders me so kind towards you. My philosophy consists in being, if possible, satisfied with myself, and in leaving the rest to go on as it may please God."

It was by passages such as the above, which abound in the Memorials against Goëzman, tha Beaumarchais managed to destroy the prejudices which had been spread against him in the public mind, to disarm the envious, convert the hostile, enlist the indifferent on his behalf, and interest every one in his cause. The page which I have just quoted appears to me one of the best as regards its naturalness, and the facility and variety of the *nuances*, above all if we add to it the following lines, which complete his answer to d'Arnaud, and, after the honey, give us the sting : " Forgive me, Sir, if I have not answered, in a letter addressed to yourself alone, all the insults in your Memorial; forgive me if, after you have measured in my heart the sombre depths of hell, and cried out : '*Thou sleepest, Jupiter; of what use, then, are thy thunderbolts ?*'—I have replied but lightly to so much inflation ; forgive me, you have been a school-boy no doubt, and you know that the best filled balloon only requires the prick of a pin."

Of all Beaumarchais' adversaries, the one he has treated worst in his Memorials, the one against whom his pen is more often carried away to excess, is the journalist Marin; but it must also be said that, of

all his enemies, this one, if not the most violent in words, was at least the most underhand, the most perfidiously venomous in his insinuations, and consequently the most irritating. When we read Marin's papers, we understand and excuse the fierceness of Beaumarchais. He was one of those *littérateurs* without talent, * who, unable to become *some one*, endeavour obstinately to become *something*, and occasionally succeed by making a great stir in gaining a sort of position; but as their reputation is based upon nothing, has no foundation, either literary or moral, it totters and crumbles to pieces at the first shock. In the first instance a schoolmaster, Marin had afterwards obtained the lucrative privilege of publishing the "Gazette de France," in which he brought those paragraphs to perfection, to which the name of an inmate of the poultry yard is at present applied, and which were then called *marinades*.†
He was moreover the censor, the head of the office of printed books, and the agent of the Chancellor Maupeou for the composition and distribution of

---

* A "History of the Sultan Saladin," written by him, is in existence: we have not read it; but to be able to affirm, without scruple, that he was destitute of talent, it is sufficient to read his Memorials against Beaumarchais, which are detestable, and some of his articles in the "Gazette de France," which are often quoted, with reason, by the Miscellanies of the time, as models of platitude.

† Marin introduced his taste for invention, even into semi-official documents. Thus, in a pretended census of the population, he had

pamphlets intended to support the new Parliaments. It was asserted that, as he liked to have several strings to his bow, he also circulated secretly the pamphlets of Maupeou's adversaries, which were very much in request and very much prohibited. He also passed, with or without reason, for an usurer, and for the director of news-offices, at which defamation was sold on the most reasonable terms. In a word, he was one of those *publicists* whose race has not perhaps entirely disappeared. He was, nevertheless, a sufficiently influential kind of personage for Voltaire to think, on one of his days of good humour, of proposing him as a candidate for the Academy: "The Gaillards," he writes to Duclos, December 22, 1770, "the Delilles, the La Harpes, are in the lists, and they have genuine qualifications; but if it is true that there will be some difficulty about the election of one of them, I recom-

almost *doubled* the figures. In allusion to this the following epigram about him was written :—

> D'une gazette ridicule
> Rédacteur faux, sot et crédule,
> Qui, bravant le sens et le goût
> Nous racontes sans nul scrupule
> Des contes à dormir debout,
> A ton dénombrement immense,
> Pour que l'on pût ajouter foi,
> Il faudrait qu'à ta ressemblance
> Chaque individu fût en France
> Soudain aussi double que toi.

mend very earnestly to your notice M. Marin, who joins to his talents the merit of continually rendering services to literary men."

The little services which Marin rendered to Voltaire consisted in introducing, in his capacity of head of the office of printed books, the works of the philosopher of Ferney, which were printed abroad and prohibited in France, and which Marin himself hawked about in the principal houses of the country. This did not prevent him from sending, by way of example, from time to time, to the galleys, poor wretches of hawkers, who were guilty of the same offence as himself. For the rest, it is edifying to observe Voltaire in his relations with this obliging correspondent. It can be seen how little inclination he had for espousing a desperate cause; for, after caressing and flattering Marin before his misfortunes, he denied him and repelled him in an outrageous manner, directly Beaumarchais' Memorials had made him a sort of infected sheep. Marin lived, at first, on sufficiently good terms with the author of "Eugénie." On hearing of the criminal action, which Goëzman was instituting against him, he had interfered, under pretext of arranging the affair; but, in the hope of pleasing the Chancellor Maupeou, he aimed at nothing less than rescuing M. and Madame Goëzman at Beaumarchais' expense, and in the following manner.—It will be

remembered, that what constituted all the strength
of the accuser was the false declaration which he
had caused Lejay the bookseller to sign. To force
the bookseller to confess the truth, Beaumarchais
depended on the evidence of Bertrand the banker,
who had negotiated the matter in his name, with
Lejay; now Bertrand, who had first of all contra-
dicted Lejay, was Marin's intimate friend, and it was
under his influence that, fearing the effects of a
contest with a member of the Parliament, he first
turned round on the main question of the fifteen
louis which had been asked for, received, and kept
by Madame Goëzman. While he at the same time
urged Bertrand to retract, Marin said to Beaumarchais: "Do not let us speak of these fifteen louis, I
will settle the affair; Lejay alone will be sacrificed."
But after Lejay had been sacrificed, and Bertrand
had retracted, Beaumarchais would have been left at
Goëzman's discretion, and such was, in his opinion,
the object of the officious journalist. "This ma-
nœuvre," said he, employing the language of Rabelais,
" was the 'joli *petit coutelet* avec lequel l'ami Marin
entendait tout *doulcettement m'égorgiller.*' "

In his first Memorial, Beaumarchais had contented
himself with warding off the blow aimed by Marin.
He did not introduce anything personal or insulting
into his statement of facts. Marin, convinced, like

Bertrand and d'Arnaud, that the accused was lost, and that the best means of imposing silence upon him was by frightening him, replied in one of the most insulting Memorials. While Bertrand the speculator borrowed his epigraph from the Psalms, Marin the journalist, who had written a history of Saladin, and doubtless prided himself on being an orientalist, displayed at the top of his paper a Persian maxim from the Poet Sadi: "Give not thy rice to the serpent, for the serpent will sting thee." Beaumarchais is the serpent; but Beaumarchais will soon prove, in his own way, that it is Marin, "who instead of giving his rice to the serpent, takes its skin, envelops himself in it, and crawls with as much ease as if he had never done anything else in his life." To sign his first Memorial, conjointly with himself, as the law demanded, Beaumarchais had only been able to find a poor, obscure advocate, named Malbête. Marin, who aims at wit, takes advantage of the circumstance, and opens with the following sentence : "A libel has been distributed at all the gates of Paris, and sold publicly, bearing the signature, Beaumarchais-Malbête." This was neat enough, but it was imprudent; for the journalist, in making this point, was venturing upon a kind of war, in which his adversary was an acknowledged master. Accordingly, a reply in the same tone, but with more smartness, was not long coming.

"The Gazetier de France complains of the falseness
of the calumnies circulated in a paper which he says
is signed Beaumarchais-Malbête, and he undertakes
to justify himself by a little manifesto, signed Marin,
qui n'est pas Malbéte."

If Marin's Memorials were merely full of plati-
tudes, Beaumarchais might be taxed with cruelty in
his replies, but they are full of a hypocritical malice, which is revolting. Marin assumes the air of a
sensitive man, deploring the ingratitude of an old
friend. In allusion to the La Blache law-suit, which
Beaumarchais had just lost, he expresses himself as
follows: "He lost this action, which compromised
so remarkably his honour and his fortune; he informed me of this mishap, I was affected by it,
and hastened to offer him in his prison the only
aid which was in my power—that of sympathising
with him and consoling him. He at last obtained
his liberty, came to thank me for my attention,
and, although there were several persons at my
house, behaved with his usual indiscretion, and
allowed himself to make remarks, which were more
than imprudent, both against his reporter, against
his opponent, and against . . . ." (The
worthy Marin here puts several dots: which means
*against the Parliament and against the Govern-
ment.*) He then continues as follows: "I was hurt
by it on account of my friendship, of which I thought

him worthy, and I reproached him with it." This, it is seen, was political denunciation, effected basely by means of insinuation and reticence. Denunciations of this kind abound in Marin's Memorials: "Ah, if I was capable of taking advantage of those effusions which friendship explains, pardons, and forgets . . . . . ." (Here come points again.) "He does not remember, then, the conversation he held at my house and elsewhere, in the presence of several witnesses, and which would procure him a punishment somewhat more severe than that which he may incur from the decision in the present case." Kind and sensitive Marin! the punishment by which Beaumarchais is threatened is *omnia citra mortem!* In another Memorial, indeed, he says with naïveté, "When the calumny circulated in a libel injures the reputation of an honest citizen, those who are its authors ought to be subjected to the severest punishments; *often even to capital punishment.*" Accordingly, he takes care to repeat, incessantly, that Beaumarchais speaks of ministers and persons in office with a boldness to be punished; that he attacks the church and the magistracy; that if he, Marin, were not too kind to profit by his advantages, he could prove with the greatest facility that his adversary had committed atrocious crimes, and that he was the worst of reprobates; "but it is not," he says, "in my disposition to do evil to my own enemies." This perfidious attitude of a man, who endeavours to stab men from behind while pretending to spare them, excited the indignation of the public, who were observing the contest; and when Beaumarchais was seen to advance resolutely against the sycophant, to attack him face to face, and overwhelm him with rapid and vigorous blows, he was applauded furiously; he was even pardoned, when, after he had felled him, he trampled him under-foot without mercy.

Every one has read the fine opening of the fourth Memorial, the most remarkable of all, in which the author, discovering the means of reviving, with more harm than ever, a subject which seemed exhausted, imagines Providence saying to him, " I am that by which everything is; without me you would not exist ; I endowed you with a healthy and robust body, in which I placed a most active mind; you know with what profusion I have poured feeling into your heart and gaiety into your disposition; but, full as you are of the happiness of thinking, of feeling, you would be too happy without some grief to counterbalance your good fortune: accordingly, you are to be overwhelmed beneath innumerable calamities, torn to pieces by a thousand enemies, deprived of your liberty and your goods, accused of robbery, forgery, bribery, and calumny, to groan beneath the opprobrium of a criminal prosecution, to be bound in the chains of a judicial sentence, attacked at every point of your existence by the most absurd rumours, and thrown upon the public, for a considerable time, for it to canvas your character and decide whether you are not the vilest of men, or only an honest citizen." Beaumarchais prostrates himself, submits humbly to the decrees of Providence, begs that he may be granted at least such enemies as may exercise his courage without confounding him, and starts from this point to pass them once more in review and give their portraits in full. We will only quote the paragraphs in which he asks Providence to give him Marin for his enemy. " I should desire," he says, " the intellect of this man to be heavy and dull; I should desire his stupid malice to have long procured for him two things, which until his time had been considered incompatible : public hatred and public contempt. I would ask, above all, that, unfaithful to his acquaintances, ungrateful to his friends, odious to authors in his censorship, nauseating to readers in his writings, terrible to borrowers in his usury, hawking about forbidden books, acting as a spy on persons who receive him into their society, plundering strangers who entrust their affairs to him, tyrannising over unfortunate booksellers in order to enrich himself, he should be such a man, that in public opinion it would be sufficient to be accused by him in order to be presumed honest, to be supported by him in order to be at once suspected: give me Marin."

The reader will, perhaps, not be displeased to hear what Marin thought of this passage. He called upon the Parliament for the author's head, not exactly on account of the insult offered to himself: he is too disinterested to care about that: but because M. Caron "insults the Divinity by a shocking impre- cation and an impious jest." At the end of his petition, he lays particular stress on the "sacrilegious prayer offered up by M. Caron to the Divinity, in which he asks him to co-operate with him in the commission of crimes. It is a licence," he adds, " of which there has been no example since the existence of the monarchy." In this manner Marin justifies his adversary in applying to him Boileau's two verses on Cotin:

" Qui méprise Marin n'estime point son roi,
Et n'a, selon Marin, ni Dieu, ni foi, ni loi."

The second portrait of Marin, which is found in the same Memorial, is more fully developed and more highly coloured; but it is exaggerated, and in some parts borders upon bad taste. Beaumarchais allows himself to get intoxicated by the applause of the pub- lic, and appeals too much to it.* The fact is, the un-

* The Provençal interrogation, ques-a-co? (what is that?) which terminates the second portrait of Marin the Provençal, and which

fortunate "Gazetier de France" came out of the struggle mortally wounded; he never recovered from it. Wherever he showed himself he was assailed with ridicule. All the little theatres profited by the vogue of the caricatures which were directed against him.* Before long the ministry, enlightened

was, it appears, his favourite expression, was considered so amusing by the Dauphine, afterwards the Queen Marie-Antoinette, who constantly repeated it, that her milliner determined to give the name of *ques-a-co* to a new head-dress consisting of a plume of feathers, which women wore on the top of the head. "This head-dress," says Bachaumont, "perpetuates the opprobrium of Marin, who is mocked even in costume."

* Let us quote, in reference to this subject, an unpublished letter from a man who had much celebrity in the eighteenth century as a burlesque writer, which induces me to give him a place in a note. It proceeds from the famous Taconet, who was an author and actor at the "Theatre de Nicolet," and who, on sending to Beaumarchais one of his pieces, wrote him the following letter, which shows at the same time the licence of the little theatres of the day, and the lively sensation which the Goëzman law-suit was producing in all classes of society:—"This, Sir," writes Taconet, "is the motive which induces me to take the liberty of offering you my little piece.— The actor who played the coachman in it having arrived at the interrogation, *En veau ?* (p. 8), added to his part, 'En veau Marin !' which was much applauded; and the same thing occurred when he came to the word, '*vache*,' and said '*En vache Goëzman*,' affecting to speak German, in allusion to the Swiss cows, whose milk has acquired a great reputation, above all, since the journalists have spoken of it. The piece went on as far as the fourth scene, in which Lisette says—
"' Mon cher Guillot, laissons ces mauvais caractères ;'
"The actress added,
"' Les Marins ne sont pas faits pour être sur terre.'
"The idea is not bad; as for the rhyme, it is not correct by more

apparently as to some of his misdeeds, deprived
him of all his places, and his fall was as rapid as his
elevation.   However, as he had contrived to gain
money, he took the philosophical resolution of with-
drawing to his native place, La Ciotat,* where he
bought the office of Lieutenant-General of the Ad-
miralty.   After the revolution, when the recollection
of his disgrace had been effaced by far more important events, he returned to Paris, where he died in
1809, in the ninetieth year of his age—the father of
literature. He had still time to see the first general
edition of the works of his terrible enemy appear.
He, doubtless, did not deserve all the disagreeable
results which ensued from his dispute with Beaumarchais; it is always necessary to allow on each side
something for exaggeration, and even for calumny,
in these desperate duels with the pen, which happily
are scarcely tolerated in the present state of society;
but it is very certain that Marin took the initiative
in the insult, and if the polemics of his adversary
sometimes shock our taste, in his own he often appears
in the sinister character of informer and hypocrite,
which renders him far from interesting.

Amongst all the unfavourable testimony against

than one letter. Moreover, there is no *s* in Marin, consequently, as a
celebrated man has said, 'all is well.' I hope, Sir, that you will forgive my importunity; I had no intention but that of declaring myself
most respectfully, &c.   "TACONET."

* In the Bouches-du-Rhône.

lassification, and which could no more have been
orrowed then, than they could be imitated now;
but, since Marin's ridiculous hypothesis has sometimes been reproduced, and since I have before me
the rough copies themselves of Beaumarchais' Memorial, I will enter into some details as to the manner
in which they were composed. We are gratified at
finding, in M. Sainte-Beuve's " Port-Royal," exact
particulars respecting the composition of the " Provincial Letters." The Memorials against Goëzman,
although of a less elevated character, are not without
some analogy to Pascal's celebrated work, as to the
composition, the publication, and the effect produced.
Like the " Provincial Letters," they embrace a great
variety of subjects. Independently of the pictures
of manners, the portraits, and the personal attacks,
we meet with discussions on private and public
rights, arguments on legal points, strictures on the
organisation of the tribunals of the period, historic
and political views; they even contain a dissertation
on baptism, in which Beaumarchais quotes Marcus
Aurelius and Tertullian, and assumes the severe
style appropriate to the subject, while he excuses
himself for being obliged to devote, as he says, his
unequal and *profane* pen to so weighty a question;
there is everything, in fine, in these Memorials,
there is even a little surgery, if only in the setting
forth of the amusing theory about Bertrand's '

apparently as to some of his misdeeds, deprived
him of all his places, and his fall was as rapid as his
elevation.   However, as he had contrived to gain
money, he took the philosophical resolution of with-
drawing to his native place, La Ciotat,* where he
bought the office of Lieutenant-General of the Ad-
miralty.   After the revolution, when the recollection
of his disgrace had been effaced by far more important events, he returned to Paris, where he died in
1809, in the ninetieth year of his age—the father of
literature. He had still time to see the first general
edition of the works of his terrible enemy appear.
He, doubtless, did not deserve all the disagreeable
results which ensued from his dispute with Beaumarchais; it is always necessary to allow on each side
something for exaggeration, and even for calumny,
in these desperate duels with the pen, which happily
are scarcely tolerated in the present state of society;
but it is very certain that Marin took the initiative
in the insult, and if the polemics of his adversary
sometimes shock our taste, in his own he often appears
in the sinister character of informer and hypocrite,
which renders him far from interesting.

Amongst all the unfavourable testimony against

than one letter. Moreover, there is no *s* in Marin, consequently, as a
celebrated man has said, 'all is well.'   I hope, Sir, that you will forgive my importunity; I had no intention but that of declaring myself
most respectfully, &c.   "TACONET."

* In the Bouches-du-Rhône.

him contained in the packet relating to the Goëzman law-suit, there is one document which deserves special mention, on account of the interest attached to the name of the witness. In his third Memorial, Beaumarchais, opposing to the eulogiums which Marin bestows on himself the complaints of various other persons, said to him—"Would you dare to depend on the testimony of M. de Saint-P., who for five years has been pining under the misfortune of having empowered you to represent him in an arbitration case; and who does not cease to call upon the ministry for vengeance on you?"

This *Saint-P.* is no other than Bernardin de Saint-Pierre, who was then vegetating in Paris, poor and unknown, and who, having been injured by Marin, replied to Beaumarchais' questions, in reference to that journalist, by an unpublished letter, from which I extract the following passage :—

"I pity you, Sir, for having found, across your path, a man so profoundly perfidious, and who can derive special power from an Inspector of Police, his friend, named d'Hémery. . . . . I hope, for the public welfare, for my own repose, and for the advantage of literature, that your affair may have the effect of throwing light on the proceedings of these people. It appears that I am wanted to offer my aid as an avenger; but I repeat, Sir, I have thrown myself upon the justice and the scrupulous honour of M. de Sartines. The day he opens his mouth to me, I will speak in the least obscure terms, and it will be impossible not to recognise the characteristics of the honourable man and the good citizen

apparently as to some of his misdeeds, deprived
him of all his places, and his fall was as rapid as his
elevation.   However, as he had contrived to gain
money, he took the philosophical resolution of with-
drawing to his native place, La Ciotat,* where he
bought the office of Lieutenant-General of the Ad-
miralty.   After the revolution, when the recollection
of his disgrace had been effaced by far more important events, he returned to Paris, where he died in
1809, in the ninetieth year of his age—the father of
literature. He had still time to see the first general
edition of the works of his terrible enemy appear.
He, doubtless, did not deserve all the disagreeable
results which ensued from his dispute with Beaumarchais; it is always necessary to allow on each side
something for exaggeration, and even for calumny,
in these desperate duels with the pen, which happily
are scarcely tolerated in the present state of society;
but it is very certain that Marin took the initiative
in the insult, and if the polemics of his adversary
sometimes shock our taste, in his own he often appears
in the sinister character of informer and hypocrite,
which renders him far from interesting.

Amongst all the unfavourable testimony against

than one letter. Moreover, there is no *s* in Marin, consequently, as a
celebrated man has said, 'all is well.' I hope, Sir, that you will forgive my importunity; I had no intention but that of declaring myself
most respectfully, &c.   'TACONET."

* In the Bouches-du-Rhône.

him contained in the packet relating to the Goëzman law-suit, there is one document which deserves special mention, on account of the interest attached to the name of the witness. In his third Memorial, Beaumarchais, opposing to the eulogiums which Marin bestows on himself the complaints of various other persons, said to him—"Would you dare to depend on the testimony of M. de Saint-P., who for five years has been pining under the misfortune of having empowered you to represent him in an arbitration case; and who does not cease to call upon the ministry for vengeance on you?"

This *Saint-P.* is no other than Bernardin de Saint-Pierre, who was then vegetating in Paris, poor and unknown, and who, having been injured by Marin, replied to Beaumarchais' questions, in reference to that journalist, by an unpublished letter, from which I extract the following passage:—

"I pity you, Sir, for having found, across your path, a man so profoundly perfidious, and who can derive special power from an Inspector of Police, his friend, named d'Hémery. . . . . . I hope, for the public welfare, for my own repose, and for the advantage of literature, that your affair may have the effect of throwing light on the proceedings of these people. It appears that I am wanted to offer my aid as an avenger; but I repeat, Sir, I have thrown myself upon the justice and the scrupulous honour of M. de Sartines. The day he opens his mouth to me, I will speak in the least obscure terms, and it will be impossible not to recognise the characteristics of the honourable man and the good citizen

apparently as to some of his misdeeds, deprived
him of all his places, and his fall was as rapid as his
elevation.   However, as he had contrived to gain
money, he took the philosophical resolution of with-
drawing to his native place, La Ciotat,* where he
bought the office of Lieutenant-General of the Ad-
miralty.   After the revolution, when the recollection
of his disgrace had been effaced by far more important events, he returned to Paris, where he died in
1809, in the ninetieth year of his age—the father of
literature.   He had still time to see the first general
edition of the works of his terrible enemy appear.
He, doubtless, did not deserve all the disagreeable
results which ensued from his dispute with Beaumarchais; it is always necessary to allow on each side
something for exaggeration, and even for calumny,
in these desperate duels with the pen, which happily
are scarcely tolerated in the present state of society;
but it is very certain that Marin took the initiative
in the insult, and if the polemics of his adversary
sometimes shock our taste, in his own he often appears
in the sinister character of informer and hypocrite,
which renders him far from interesting.

Amongst all the unfavourable testimony against

than one letter. Moreover, there is no *s* in Marin, consequently, as a
celebrated man has said, 'all is well.' I hope, Sir, that you will forgive my importunity ; I had no intention but that of declaring myself
most respectfully, &c.   "TACONET."

* In the Bouches-du-Rhône.

him contained in the packet relating to the Goëzman law-suit, there is one document which deserves special mention, on account of the interest attached to the name of the witness. In his third Memorial, Beaumarchais, opposing to the eulogiums which Marin bestows on himself the complaints of various other persons, said to him—"Would you dare to depend on the testimony of M. de Saint-P., who for five years has been pining under the misfortune of having empowered you to represent him in an arbitration case; and who does not cease to call upon the ministry for vengeance on you?"

This *Saint-P.* is no other than Bernardin de Saint-Pierre, who was then vegetating in Paris, poor and unknown, and who, having been injured by Marin, replied to Beaumarchais' questions, in reference to that journalist, by an unpublished letter, from which I extract the following passage :—

"I pity you, Sir, for having found, across your path, a man so profoundly perfidious, and who can derive special power from an Inspector of Police, his friend, named d'Hémery. . . . . I hope, for the public welfare, for my own repose, and for the advantage of literature, that your affair may have the effect of throwing light on the proceedings of these people. It appears that I am wanted to offer my aid as an avenger; but I repeat, Sir, I have thrown myself upon the justice and the scrupulous honour of M. de Sartines. The day he opens his mouth to me, I will speak in the least obscure terms, and it will be impossible not to recognise the characteristics of the honourable man and the good citizen

"What is marked out at the bottom of the fourth page, appears absolutely superfluous and disgusting.*

"What is marked out in the fifth, might have been written by Baculard; the exordium is considered too long. We are all agreed that at all events this paragraph ought to be shortened.

"The first paragraph of the seventh page does not appear clear unless you mark out *pour bien prouver ce que je n'ai fait qu'avancer*, and substitute in that case, *ne plus revenir* instead of *me taire.* The sentence will then be as follows :—' What remains for me to do? To say no more about what I have proved, to prove what I have only advanced, and to reply in short to a number of Memorials, &c.'"

Beaumarchais takes advantage, in the most docile manner, of all these criticisms ; accordingly his Memorials against Goëzman, if from the nature of the subject they do not offer all the interest of "The Barber of Seville" and "The Marriage of Figaro," are nevertheless, as regards style, the most remarkable of all his works, and those in which the fine qualities of the writer are most free from any admixture of faults. There are some passages of a most finished perfection. At a later period, after his great successes on the stage, Beaumarchais became less accessible to criticism. We shall see the consequences in the Kornman law-suit. During the period at which we have at present arrived, he turned everything to account, even

* It appears that his friends went so far as to take the liberty of marking out, provisionally, whatever displeased them in his manuscript.

the prose of his sister Julie: for instance, they composed together that passage in the Memorials, which is sometimes quoted with reason as one of the most graceful, in which the writer replies to the attacks of Madame Goëzman on the subject of the birth and profession of his father; the original text, instead of being too copious, as was generally the case, was, on the contrary, somewhat barren :—

"I confess," replied Beaumarchais, "that nothing can absolve me from the very grave reproach which you address to me of being the son of my father: it is true I know of no other for whom I would change him. . But I am too well acquainted with the value of time, which he taught me to measure, to lose it in taking up such insipidities."

Julie thinking, no doubt, that this was deficient in colour, suggested a different treatment and wrote the passage with her own hand twice over, on a separate sheet of paper :—

"You commence," writes Julie, "this masterpiece, by reproaching me with the profession of my father, *with his having been a watchmaker: Oh! what excellent humour. And you fought it is said with Marin, in order to rob him of this point, which he had appropriated.* * Well, Monsieur and Madame, it is true that to several other branches of commerce he united

---

* The free turn of Julie's style is at once recognised; but the tone was here too familiar, and it will be seen that Beaumarchais suppressed, very justly, the italicised portion of the sentence.

a sufficiently great celebrity in the art of watchmaking : forced to submit to condemnation on this point, I confess, with grief, that nothing can absolve me from the very grave reproach which you address to me of being the son of my father; but I pause; for *stay*, I perceive that he is behind me reading what I write, and he smiles while he embraces me, as if delighted that I belonged to him."

It is evident that the original sketch has acquired colour and animation under Julie's pen ; her brother has only to give it the final touch, and he does so very cleverly, for here is the text as it at last stood, and as it was published :—

"You spoil this masterpiece by reproaching me with the profession of my ancestors. Alas! Madame, it is too true that the last of all of them united to several other branches of commerce a sufficiently great celebrity in the art of watchmaking. Forced to submit to condemnation on this point, I confess, with grief, that nothing can absolve me from the very just reproach, which you address to me, of being the son of my father. . . . . But I pause, for I perceive that he is behind me, looking at what I write, and he smiles as he embraces me. O you, who reproach me with my father, you have no idea of his generous heart. In truth, watchmaking apart, I know of none for whom I would change him. But I am too well acquainted with the value of time, which he taught me to measure, to lose it in taking up such insipidities."

The picture thus completed and re-touched is perfect as regards tone and shade, but it is incontestable that the happiest idea came from Julie. Perhaps, also, this idea had been inspired by old M. Caron himself, whom we can imagine, naturally enough, assisting at the composition and putting his white head over the shoulders of the pair. This passage is otherwise almost the only one in which the style of another person is mixed up, to a certain extent, with that of Beaumarchais. The Memorials, then, are entirely his own. What he borrows from Julie even does not count; for, in appropriating his sister's wit, Beaumarchais could still say, that it was all in the family.

It now only remains for us to endeavour to represent the attitude of the public in this struggle between a private individual and a detested parliament, which they identified with Goëzman. In reckoning on the assistance he might derive from circumstances, the intrepid suitor had not been wrong. After the appearance of this second Memorial, his cause had become, as was said at the time, the cause of the nation, and he found himself the object of a perpetually increasing sympathy. This was kept up by the very duration of the contest, the result of which was retarded by a variety of incidents, and delayed for seven months, from August 1773, till February 1774. During these seven months, in the absence of more important events, the eyes of all Paris, France, we may even say Europe, were fixed upon Beaumarchais and his law-suit.

It is known with what ardent curiosity and interest

Voltaire followed this affair from his retreat at Ferney. Although he had at first sided with the chancellor Maupeou, he now deserted the ministerial flag, and underwent the influence of Beaumarchais' Memorials.

"What a man!" he writes to D'Alembert; "he unites everything—humour, seriousness, argument, gaiety, force, pathos, every kind of eloquence, and he seeks for none, and he confounds all his adversaries, and he gives lessons to his judges. His naïveté enchants me. I forgive him his imprudence and his petulance."

"I am afraid," he says elsewhere, "that this brilliant, hare-brained fellow is at bottom right in spite of every one. What roguery, oh heaven! What horrors! What degradation in the country! What a shock for the Parliament!" * The phlegmatic Horace Walpole, although less affected than Voltaire, also yields to the influence of the Memorials. "I have received," he writes, to Madame du Deffand, "Beaumarchais' 'Memorials;' I am at the third volume, and they amuse me very much. The man is very skilful; he reasons correctly, and has a great

* *Vide* Voltaire's correspondence from Dec. 1773 to April 1774, in which he speaks incessantly of Beaumarchais. If La Harpe is to be believed, he even thought of him so much as to experience some jealousy, for he is said to have written as follows, in reference to the Memorials:—"They exhibit much wit; I think, however, that more is required to write 'Zaïre and Mérope.'" This sentence, quoted by La Harpe, is not found in the published correspondence.

deal of wit; his pleasantry is sometimes very good; but he delights in it too much. In fine, I can understand, considering the party spirit at present among you, this affair causing a great sensation. I was forgetting to tell you with what horror your mode of administering justice struck me. Is there a country in the world, in which this Madame Goëzman would not have been severely punished? Her deposition is shameless to a fearful extent. Are persons allowed then with you to lie, to prevaricate, to contradict themselves, to abuse their opponents in in so desperate a manner? What has become of this creature and her villanous husband? Answer me, I beseech you!"*

In Germany, the effect was not less than in England. Göthe has related to us, himself, how at Frankfort, in a circle where Beaumarchais' Memorials were being read aloud, a young girl gave him the idea of transforming the Clavijo episode into a drama.† At Paris, the impression they produced was naturally still stronger; Goëzman's adversary had for him not only all the young men and women, but all the former advocates of the ancient Parliament, and all their connections. Even more, for such was the levity of mind in official regions, that

* *Vide* Madame du Deffand's letters to Horace Walpole, vol. iii., p. 90, edition of 1812.

† *Vide* Göthe's Autobiography.

Louis XV. himself found amusement in the work ; it made Madame du Barry laugh, and she had "proverbs" played at her house, in which the confrontation of Madame Goëzman with Beaumarchais was represented on the stage. Maupeou alone did not laugh when he thought of the consequences of this success, disastrous as it was to a scheme which had cost him so many efforts, and had exposed him to so much animosity. The enthusiasm which this judicial comedy then excited, is expressed in a lively manner in the two following letters, which were addressed to Beaumarchais by the wife of one of the Presidents of the old Parliament, Madame de Meinières ; * they contain moreover a witty analysis of the fourth Memorial, which determines me to give them almost entire :—

"I have finished this astonishing Memorial, Sir. Yesterday, I cursed the visits which interrupted me in such delightful reading, although when the persons had gone, I thanked them for having prolonged my pleasure by interrupting it. Blessed, on the contrary, for ever be the '*grand cousin*,' the '*sacristan*,' the '*publicist*,' and all the worthies who have called forth the narrative of your journey to Spain. You ought to reward these persons. Your best friends could not have put you in so good a light by their eulogiums and their affection, as your enemies have done by forcing you to speak of yourself. Grandison, the most perfect hero of a romance,

---

* Madame de Meinières had a certain literary reputation. She had translated Hume's "History of England."

does not reach up to your ankle. When we follow you to this M. Clavijo's, to M. Whall's, in the park of Aranjuèz, to the ambassador's, to the king's, we become as anxious, as excited, and as indignant as yourelf. What a magic pencil is yours, Sir! what energy of thought and expression! what rapidity of wit! what an incredible compound of warmth and prudence, courage and sensibility, genius and grace! I had the honour to see Mademoiselle d'Ossun,* yesterday, and we spoke of you and your Memorial; what else can be spoken of? She told me that you had called upon her. If you want to see her, she comes pretty regularly, every Sunday, to the Pavilions, † and I offer to bring you together there. She is a girl of the greatest merit, whose head and heart are excellent; but *apropos* of heart and head, what were you doing with them at Madame de Saint Jean's? You appeared to be displaying all the qualities of an agreeable man, which is not the way to be most attractive to an old woman like me. I saw, well enough, that you possessed wit, talent, confidence, and the art of pleasing in conversation; but I should never have perceived in you, Sir, a true father of a family, and the sublime author of your four Memorials. ‡ I must be very stupid, and the points which compose the brilliancy of a circle, like that of this charming woman, must dazzle and fatigue a savage of my kind, so as to prevent her distinguishing them.

* The sister of the Marquis d'Ossun, the French Ambassador in Spain, who had been very obliging to Beaumarchais during his stay at Madrid.

† The Pavilions of Chaillot.

‡ This sentence shows what a feeling of surprise the Memorials produced on those who had hitherto only known Beaumarchais as a very gay and somewhat foppish man of the world; "ayant," (to employ the delicate and polite expression of Madame de Meinières), "de la *confiance.*"

"Receive my thanks for the enthusiasm which you excite in your readers, and the assurance of the genuine esteem with which

"I have the honour to be, Sir, &c.,

"GUICHARD DE MEINIERES.

"18th February, 1774."

"Whatever be the result of your quarrel with so many adversaries, I congratulate you, Sir, on having had it; it will, in any case, prove that you are one of the most honourable men in the world, since, after searching through your life, it has been impossible to show that you are a villain, and assuredly you have made yourself known as a most eloquent man, in every kind of eloquence belonging to this century. Your prayer to the Supreme Being is a masterpiece of the sublime and the comic; the astounding, ingenious, novel intermixture of which produces the greatest effect. I confess with Madame Goëzman, that you are somewhat *malin;* and following her example, I forgive you, for your *malices* are delightful. I hope, Sir, you have not a sufficiently bad opinion of me, to pity me for reading a hundred and eight pages, when they are written by you. I begin by devouring them, then I retrace my steps; I stop now at a passage worthy of Demosthenes, now at another, superior to Cicero, and at last, at a thousand, as humourous as Molière; I am so afraid of finishing and being unable to read anything else afterwards, that I recommence each paragraph to give you enough time to produce your fifth Memorial, in which we shall no doubt find your confrontation with M. Goëzman; I must only beg of you to do me the favour to give me notice the night before the bookseller sends copies to the widow La Marche; she is the person who has always supplied them to me. I take several of them at a time, for ourselves and for *our friends ;** and I am enraged, when, from not know-

---

* *Our friends* were the members of the old Parliament.

ing they have appeared, I send too late, and am told in reply that I must wait until the following day."

There was a general rivalry as to who should send Beaumarchais information, advice, congratulations, and encouragement. Many persons even carried their good intentions so far as to send him, in their modesty, Memorials ready written, as if his wit could not do without their assistance. One of these correspondents, who did not sign his name, but who appears to me to have been a member of the old Parliament, sent him the plan of a Memorial, impressed upon him the necessity of secrecy, and terminated as follows: "The machine is coming to pieces, thanks to you. Is not this the time for striking the grand blow? I refer it all to your prudence. From your writings I think you as honest a man as myself, which I would not say of every one; I fear nothing." And the letter is without a signature! What a Bayard is this correspondent! The world is full of these heroic persons who exhort others to deeds of daring from beneath the veil of the anonymous.

Beaumarchais was not wanting in audacity, but he did not wish to drive the Parliament to extremities; he knew that public favour was fleeting and inconstant. The Prince de Conti, his warmest protector, had said to him, "If you have the misfortune to come under the hands of the executioner, I shall be obliged to abandon you." What he had to do then was to preserve and maintain the power he derived from the opposition, without exasperating his judges, who were already in a state of irritation; always to suit his tone to the rank of the persons he attacked; and to be able when necessary, as has been wittily said, to strike while kneeling. This is exactly what he did, and with marvellous tact, after an incident which increased still more the interest he had already inspired. A colonel of cavalry whom Maupeou had transformed *ex abrupto* into a magistrate, the President de Nicolai, an intimate friend of Goëzman's, met Beaumarchais in the Salle des Pas Perdus, and insulted him by ordering the officers to turn him out. Beaumarchais accordingly made a complaint against the insulter. The first President sent for him, and invited him to withdraw his complaint. He consented to do so; but in his last Memorial, with external signs of respect beneath which disdain can be seen, he explains publicly why he consented to forgive M. de Nicolai. In a short time his influence became such that this suitor, who had been treated with so much contempt by his judges at the commencement of the action, and who had not been suffered to make his accusations in the ordinary legal forms, had only to point out in his Memorials those whom he considered his most violent enemies, in order to make them yield to his challenge. One of them, a councillor of the grand chamber, named Gin, addressed to him a sort of apology, six pages in length, from which I extract some passages, which show how the pride of the judge disappeared before the popularity of the accused.

"I have read your last Memorial, Sir," writes councillor Gin; "I yield to your prayers by ceasing to be your judge; but, in order to avoid all misunderstanding as to the motives, which have hitherto prevented me from taking this determination, and those which lead me to do so at present, I think I ought to inform you and the public of these motives."

And, after a long explanation of his conduct, this magistrate, who was at first Beaumarchais' declared enemy, terminates as follows :—

"I think I have proved, Sir, that I have even now all the impartiality necessary for judging M. and Madame de Goëzman and yourself; but your attacks have been so multiplied, that if I were to appear as your judge, I should have reason to fear the public might suspect me of some unfavourable feeling towards you. To this delicacy I sacrifice my individual sentiments; and in order to give you a fresh proof of my impartiality, I declare to you, Sir, that I require no other reparation for the imputations contained in your Memorials than that of *giving publicity* to this letter, which I forward, at the same time, to the first President. I am, Sir, with all the sentiments due to you,

"Your very humble, &c.

"Feb. 15, 1774."   "GIN.*

---

* This is the same magistrate who admits to Beaumarchais the influence exercised by the public rumours on his decision in the La

What a singular substitution of parts !   The judge
pleads before the accused, and the accused is about
to teach dignity to the judge, by writing on his side
to the first President a letter, from which I borrow
only the following lines :—

"Monseigneur,—I have the honour to address to you a
copy of the *apologetic* letter I have received from M. Gin.
My profound respect for the court prevents me giving this
letter the publicity which this magistrate seems at first to
have desired it should receive, convinced as I am, that when
he reflects upon it again, he will be obliged to me for re-
nouncing all idea of printing it with my commentary."

What, indeed, can be more strange than this step
of a magistrate, who himself solicits an accused
person, whose Memorials constitute an infraction of
the law, and were soon afterwards condemned to be
burnt, to grant him a place in these Memorials to

Blache suit, out of which the Goëzman suit sprang.   The admission
is worth preserving.—" Whether from reason," he writes, "*or from the
impressions which the public rumours, even though calumnious, have
left on people's minds, and from which it is difficult to keep free,* I
will not conceal from you that the combination of peculiarities connected with your deed, your letters, and all your affair, determined
me to 'support' the letters of rescission."   Councillor Gin means by
this, that he had expressed his opinion that the statement of accounts
between Paris du Verney and Beaumarchais should be declared null.
This opinion, without being substantially more advantageous for him,
was less offensive in form than that of Goëzman, which had been
adopted by the Parliament, and in virtue of which the act in question
had been declared, indirectly, to be a forgery.

justify himself with the public! Who does not recognise in this, a brilliant testimony to the power which Beaumarchais derived from public opinion, which he had contrived to gain, and which he opposed like a buckler to his enemies.

However, if fear acted on some of the magistrates of the Maupeou Parliament, hatred and fear ruled alternately in the hearts of the majority, who saw with delight the hour of vengeance approaching. The day for giving judgment arrived at last, on the 26th February 1774, amid universal expectation. " We are expecting to day," writes Madame du Deffand to Walpole, "a great event : Beaumarchais' judgment. . . . M. de Monaco has invited him this evening to read us a comedy of his composition, entitled 'The Barber of Seville.' . . . . . The public are infatuated with the author who is receiving judgment while I am writing. It is expected that the judgment will be severe, and it may happen, that instead of supping with us, he may be condemned to exile, or even to the pillory. I will tell you tomorrow."

Such is the amount of interest Madame du Deffand took in people! What a pity for her if the accused had been condemned to the pillory! She would have lost the reading of " The Barber." She did lose it, all the same; the judges deliberated for so long a time (for twelve hours) that Beaumarchais addressed to the Prince of Monaco the following unpublished letter, which forms a pendant to that of Madame du Deffand.

"Beaumarchais, infinitely sensible of the honour which the Prince de Monaco has been kind enough to do him, sends this acknowledgment from the court, where he has been kept since six in the morning, where he has been questioned at the bar, where he is waiting for his judgment, for which he has had to wait a long time; but, whatever turn affairs may take, Beaumarchais, who is surrounded by his relations at the present moment, cannot expect to escape from them, whether he has compliments of congratulation or of condolence to receive. He begs the Prince de Monaco to do him the favour of reserving his kindness for another day. He has the honour to assure him of his very respectful gratitude.

"Saturday, February 26, 1774."

When he wrote this letter, Beaumarchais, after entering the court, where he had seen all his judges pass before him, had been just submitted, according to custom, to his last interrogatory; the preceding night had been devoted by him to the settlement of his affairs. It appears that he had decided upon killing himself, in case of being condemned to the pillory.* Seeing that there was no end to the deliberation, he withdrew to the residence of Madame

---

* So, at least, it appears from a passage in one of his Memorials, in his appeal from the judgment in the La Blache case.

Lépine, his sister, went to bed, and enjoyed a profound sleep.

"He slept," says Gudin, in his manuscript, "and his judges kept awake, tormented by their anger and divided amongst themselves. They deliberated with tumult; expressed their opinions with rage; wished to punish the author of the Memorials; foresaw the clamour of the public, who were ready to disavow them, and filled the place with their cries of contention."

They at last determined upon a sentence, by which they hoped to satisfy the public and at the same time avenge themselves. They condemned Madame Goëzman to the penalty of *blame*, and ordered her to restore the fifteen louis, which were to be distributed to the poor. Her husband was placed " out of court " —a sentence which was equivalent to the other, in the case of a magistrate, and which forced him to resign his office.* Beaumarchais was also condemned to the penalty of " blame."

* This action, so imprudently commenced, and so violently followed up by Goëzman, brought misfortune to him. He lost his place and his reputation. After being sacrificed by his colleagues, he retired into obscurity; and, twenty years afterwards, I find his name on the list of persons decapitated on the 7th Thermidor, two days before the fall of Robespierre. This is plainly the man. Louis-Valentin Goëzman, formerly Councillor in the Maupeou Parliament; convicted, according to the polite formula of the time, of " having rendered himself the enemy of the people." He figured in the same cart-load with André Chénier. The Reign of Terror might well have spared Goëzman; it had plenty of more interesting men to devour, but nothing came amiss to it.

This penalty was one of infamy, and answered as nearly as possible to what is now called "civic degradation." It rendered the condemned incapable of occupying, any public function, and he had to receive his sentence on his knees before the court, the president saying to him : "The court blames thee, and declares thee infamous." Beaumarchais was awaked to hear the result :—

"He rose tranquilly," says Gudin, "equally the master of his movements and his intellect. 'Let us see,' he said, ' what there remains to be done.' We went out together to his sisters ; I did not know whether they were not waiting about the house to arrest him. I was ignorant of his designs, and did not wish to leave him. After having gone some distance, in order to be certain that he was not being followed, he took leave of me, and made an appointment with me for the next day in the asylum he had chosen; for it was to be feared that in order to carry out the sentence, the court might send for him to his own house ; but this sentence had been so ill received by the multitude assembled at the door of the chamber, the judges had been so hooted on rising, although many of them escaped by corridors which were unknown to the public, they saw so many signs of discontent, that they were not tempted to carry into execution a sentence which only drew down upon them the 'blame' of every one."

The reader knows what a brilliant triumph followed this sentence, the execution of which was prevented by Beaumarchais' popularity. All Paris called at his house, and the Prince de Conti and the Duke de Chartres, gave him a brilliant *fête*, on the morrow of

the very day on which the Tribunal had attempted
to brand him. M. de Sartines said to him, "It is
not enough for you to be 'blamed,' it is also necessary to be modest." When such discrepancies take
place in society it is much diseased. Let us add to
these particulars, which are known, one of a private
and delicate nature, which I borrow from Gudin's
manuscript :—

"He had," says Gudin, "consolations more touching still
than those of friendship. His celebrity gained for him the
attention of a woman who was endowed with a sensitive heart
and a firm disposition, fitted to sustain him in the cruel combats in which he had still to engage. She did not know him,
but her heart, moved by the perusal of his Memorials, was at-
tracted to that of this celebrated man. She desired ardently
to see him. I was with him, when, making music her pretext,
she sent a man with whom she was acquainted, and who
was also acquainted with Beaumarchais, to beg him to
lend her his harp for a few minutes. Such a request, under
such circumstances, revealed her meaning. Beaumarchais
understood it — appreciated it, and replied, 'I never lend
my harp; but if she will come with you, I will hear her,
and she can hear me.' She came—I was a witness of their
first interview. I have already said that it was difficult
to see Beaumarchais without loving him. What impression must he not have produced, when he was covered with
the applause of all Paris — when he was looked upon as
the defender of oppressed liberty—the avenger of the public.
It was still more difficult to resist the looks, the voice, the
bearing, and the conversation of this young woman; and the
attraction which each of them exercised upon the other at first
sight, increased from hour to hour, from the variety of their

charms, and the number of excellent qualities which each of
them displayed in proportion as the acquaintance increased.
Their hearts were united from this moment by a bond which
nothing could break, and which love, esteem, confidence,
time, and law rendered indissoluble.*

These popular and princely ovations, this happiness of the heart, more sweet still, doubtless repaid
Beaumarchais for the blow he had received from the
Parliament; the blow, however, was a severe one.
Indeed, the Maupeou Parliament could not long survive this act of anger and vengeance. In inflicting
civil death on a man whom public opinion carried in
triumph, it had inflicted death on itself. The sleep-
ing opposition awoke, and fell upon it with redoubled
fury. Pamphlets, in prose and verse, acquired a new
vivacity.† It lingered on for some months longer,

---

* The charming person of whom Gudin here speaks, and who became afterwards Beaumarchais' third wife, was named Marie-Thérèse
Emilie Willermawlaz. She was, as we have already said elsewhere,
of Swiss origin, and belonged to a distinguished family in Charmey.
I have seen a large portrait of her, in which she is represented with
the costume in which she perhaps appeared on the day of the interview, for she wears the famous plume of feathers à la quesaco, and
looks charming in this head-dress. Some of her letters, which we
shall quote in their proper place, will prove that she was, moreover,
a very remarkable woman, from her intellect, wit, and disposition.

† By one of those *jeux de mots*, in the Parisian taste, it was said,
in allusion to the Goëzman prosecution, " Louis Quinze destroyed the
old Parliament, quinze louis will destroy the new." Bachaumont,
without quoting it, mentions a very popular satirical ballad, in which
all the personages and incidents of this suit were introduced. I found

amid public contempt; the end of Louis XV.'s reign hastened its fall, and one of the first acts of Louis XVI. was to re-establish the old Parliament; but until the occurrence of this event, which might still have been at some distance, the terrible sentence against Beaumarchais existed with all its consequences. He found his career destroyed; two lawsuits lost at the same time, one of which had ruined him in fortune and honour, while the other, although it replaced him in public esteem, had destroyed him in a legal point of view—were weighing upon him with all their weight. He had to obtain the reconsideration of these two suits; to start with, it was necessary to obtain the reversal of the last sentence.

To apply quietly for this reversal to the Council of State, was to expose himself to almost certain refusal; to publish any fresh writings was impossible. Louis XV., although he had been sometimes amused by the Memorials against Goëzman, was nevertheless very much annoyed by the agitation produced by the discussion. He had had the dangerous suitor formally enjoined, by M. de Sartines, to preserve an absolute

this ballad among Julie's papers, and as there are two copies of it, in her hand-writing, with different readings, and as she often devoted herself to this slightly burlesque kind of poetry, I am inclined to think that she is the author of the ballad in question, which I give entire, in the Appendix No. 3. Whoever has read the Memorials against Goëzman will recognise in this song a sufficiently good caricature of all Beaumarchais' adversaries.

silence for the future; but the time allowed for ap-
pealing against the decision was slipping by, and the
sentence was about to become irrevocable.   Happily
for Beaumarchais, his fortune, always a strange one,
ordained that Louis XV., forming his opinion of him
from the very talent he had shown in the Goëzman
affair, thought he had need of him.   As kings could
then, by means of " letters of relief," relieve persons
·from the effect of the lapse of time allowed for appeals
having passed by, he promised to enable him to regain
his civil position, if he fulfilled with zeal and success
a difficult mission, to which he attached the greatest
importance — and the conqueror of the Maupeou
Parliament started for London in the capacity of
secret agent.

CHAPTER XIV.

THE history of Beaumarchais' secret mission is in-
structive, from the light it throws upon the system
of absolute government. The weak sides of free
governments have been sufficiently called attention
to during the last few years, owing to the abuse
which has been made of liberty, and the sad consequences of this abuse, to render it, perhaps, interesting for us to examine the reverse of the medal, and
study minutely what was taking place behind the
scenes of government, at a time when publicity,
discussion, and responsibility were strangers to it.
It will, perhaps, not be useless to show what importance was then attached to the most miserable trifles,
what a waste of the public money took place under
the shelter of ministerial irreponsibility, through what
complicated roads a man who had been visited with
an unjust sentence was obliged to pass, in order to

get restored to his former position; and as, on the other hand, this same man, after being sentenced to civil death by a tribunal, could become the private agent and correspondent of two kings and their ministers, and succeed, little by little, through making himself useful in small manœuvres of secret diplomacy, not only in regaining his civil rights, but also in getting an important affair, worthy of himself and his intelligence, entrusted to him, and in exercising in the shade a considerable influence, of which hitherto little has been known on a great event.

We have just left Goëzman's adversary vanquished by the Parliament, but triumphant in the eyes of public opinion, surrounded with homage, overwhelmed with congratulations, and yet sad in the midst of his triumph.

"They have delivered it at last," he wrote to a friend, some days after his condemnation; "they have at last delivered this abominable sentence, which is a masterpiece of animosity and iniquity. I am now cut off from society, and dishonoured in the midst of my career. I know, my friend, that the punishment of opinion ought not to afflict any but those who deserve it. I know that unjust judges can do everything against the person of an innocent man, and nothing against his reputation; all France have left their names at my house, since Saturday! . . . What has gone to my heart, most of all, in this fatal affair, is the bad impression of me which has been given to the king. He has been told that I was aiming at a seditious celebrity; but he has not been told that I only defended myself, and that I have not ceased to make all the magistrates feel the consequences which might result from this ridiculous prosecution. You know, my friend, that I had hitherto lived a calm and tranquil life, and I should never have written anything about political matters, if a host of powerful enemies had not combined to ruin me. Was I to allow myself to be crushed without justifying myself? If I have done so with too much hastiness, is that a reason for dishonouring my family and myself, and excluding from society an honest subject, whose talents might have been employed with utility in the service of the king and the state? I have enough strength to support a misfortune which I have not deserved; but my father, who has seventy-seven years of honours and labour over his head, and who is dying of grief, my sisters, who are women, and weak—one of whom is vomiting blood, while the other can scarcely breathe—these are the things which kill me, and for which I cannot be consoled. Receive, my generous friend, the sincere testimony of the ardent gratitude with which

" I am, &c.,

" Beaumarchais." ·

This letter, which contrasts with the state of intense delight in which we naturally represent Beaumarchais at a time when princes of the blood were calling him the "great citizen," had an object; it was addressed to the Farmer-General de La Borde, who was, at the same time, Louis XV.'s first groom of the Chamber. M. de La Borde cultivated the arts; he composed rather indifferent opera music,* he was intimate with Beaumarchais, he was much loved by the king, and defended, as best he could,

---

* He wrote the music to Voltaire's opera of " Pandore."

against the prepossessions of his master, the audacious suitor, who was then called, at the court, "the
French Wilkes," in allusion to the tribune, who, at
the same time, was getting up agitations in England.

It will be remembered that Louis XV. had imposed an absolute silence on Beaumarchais, which
prevented him making any effectual application
for a reversal of his sentence. One day, when
speaking of the latter with La Borde, he said to him,
" It is asserted that your friend has great talent for
negotiation; if he could be employed with success
and secrecy in a matter which interests me, his
affairs would profit by it." Now the following was the
grave subject which gave uneasiness to the old king.

There was then in London an adventurer from
Burgundy, named Théveneau de Morande, who, to
escape the consequences of the disorderly life he had
led in his own country, had taken refuge in England,
where, finding himself without resources, he dealt in
scandal, and composed gross libels, which were introduced clandestinely into France, and in which he
defamed, insulted, and calumniated, without distinction, all names, if ever so little known, which came
under his pen. Amongst other works, he had published, under the impudent title of "The Journalist
in Armour," * a collection of atrocities which perfectly corresponded with the impudence of his title.

* "Le Gazetier cuirassé."

Profiting by the fear he inspired, he from time to time sent applications for money, across the channel, to those who were afraid of his attacks. It appears, even, that he attempted to obtain hush money from Voltaire, but without success; the philosopher of Ferney was not to be frightened by so little, and he contented himself with inflicting publicly on "The Journalist in Armour," the expression of his contempt: Morande, in a word, was pursuing, with less celebrity, the trade which, in the sixteenth century, had made Aretino surnamed the "Scourge of Princes." To a practitioner of this kind Madame du Barry was a gold mine; accordingly, he had written to this lady to announce to her the forthcoming publication, except in case of a handsome bonus, of an interesting work, founded upon her life and of which he sent her the prospectus, bearing the following very attractive title for a certain class of amateurs: "Mémoires secrets d'une femme publique." Any other person than Madame du Barry, might have disdained the insults of this pamphleteer, or have prosecuted him in the English courts; it can be understood that Madame du Barry was not able to take either of these courses; alarmed and enraged, she communicated her anger and her fear to Louis XV., who began by applying to the King of England for Morande's extradition. The English Government replied that, if it was not desired to prosecute this libeller, it would offer no opposition to the removal of a man who was so unworthy of the protection of the English laws, but that it could not take part in his removal, and that it could not even permit it, except on one condition: that it should be accomplished with the greatest secrecy, and in such a manner as not to wound the susceptibility of the national character. The French ministry accordingly sent a brigade of police agents to London, to seize Morande secretly; but the latter was cunning and active: he had correspondents in Paris, occupying, perhaps, high positions, who had warned him of the expedition, and, not content with taking measures for rendering it abortive, he had denounced it in the London journals, at the same time, giving himself out as a political exile, whom his persecutors dared to follow, even on to the soil of liberty, thus for the sake of an ignoble trade, violating the generous hospitality which England grants so nobly to the vanquished of all parties. The English public became excited; and when the French police agents arrived, they were pointed out to the people, who felt it their duty to throw them into the Thames. They had only time to conceal themselves, and went back as quickly as possible, very much frightened, and swearing they would never be caught at such a thing again.

Proud of this success, Morande hastened the publication of the scandalous work he had prepared. Three thousand copies were printed, and ready to be sent off to Holland and Germany, to be afterwards circulated throughout France. Being no longer able to get the author into his power, Louis XV. had sent different agents to treat with him: but Morande kept himself on the *qui vive*, would not allow any one to approach him, and, although nothing but a shame-less adventurer, assumed before the English people, the character of an avenger of public morality. Such was the state of things when the king, having exhausted his means, proposed to Beaumarchais through M.de la Borde, to start for London, to treat with the "Journalist in Armour," and purchase his silence and the destruction of his "Memoirs of Madame du Barry." A mission to protect the honour of a woman who had so little to protect as Madame du Barry, was not, it must be admitted, one of a very high order; but, besides the fact that in this case the interest of the King of France, was unfortunately mixed up with that of his too celebrated mistress, we must, before casting the stone at Beaumarchais, take a just view of his situation. It must be remembered that after being branded with disgrace by magistrates of no reputation, and who had been judges in their own case, he found his only means of reinstating himself para-lysed by the express order of an all-powerful king,

who could open or shut to him the roads by which
the reversal of the sentence was to be obtained;
who could restore to him his credit, his fortune, and
his civil rights; and this all-powerful king was
asking him a personal service, and assuring him of
his gratitude if he performed it. The period at
which we live is, without doubt, infinitely praiseworthy from the austerity of its principles, and,
above all, of its practices. However, it is not
very evident to us that under similar circumstances
no one could be found to run after the mission
which Beaumarchais contented himself with accepting. The brilliant writer accordingly went to
London, in March 1774, and, as the celebrity of his
real name might have interfered with the success of
his operations, he took the false one of Ronac, an
anagram of Caron. In a few days he had gained
the confidence of the libel-writer, had completed a
negotiation which had been dragging on for eighteen
months, and, reappearing at Versailles with a copy of
the Memoirs which caused so much alarm, and the
manuscript of another libel by the same author,
received the king's orders for a final arrangement.
Louis XV., surprised at the rapidity of his success,
expressed his satisfaction to him, and referred him to
the Duke d'Aiguillon to arrange about Morande's
terms. The minister, who was violently attacked in the
libel, cared much less about destroying it than about

ascertaining exactly what the author's connections were in France. Hence arose a scene with Beaumarchais, which does honour to him, and which we must reproduce, in order to show how he understood, and what limits he assigned to, the unenviable part which his situation caused him to accept.

"Too happy," writes Beaumarchais, in an unpublished paper, addressed to Louis XVI., after the death of his predecessor, "too happy to succeed in suppressing these libels without their being made a means of casting suspicion on all persons who may happen to be displeasing, I refused to play the infamous part of informer, to become the instrument of a perhaps general prosecution, and to light up a war of bastilles and dungeons. The Duke d'Aiguillon in his anger communicated my refusal to the king; his majesty, before condemning me, wished to know my reasons. I had the courage to reply that I could find means of putting the king beyond uneasiness with regard to all kinds of libels, both for the present and the future, but that I should think I was dishonouring myself completely, if, on the false indication or perfidious confession of a man of such bad repute as the author, I were to accuse in France, persons who perhaps had had no more connection than myself with those unworthy productions. Finally, I begged the king not to entrust me with this odious commission, for which I was less fitted than any one. The king consented to yield to my reasons; but the Duke d'Aiguillon retained a resentment towards me for my refusal, of which he gave me the most insulting proofs on the occasion of my second journey. I was so disheartened, that, without a very particular order from the king, I should have given it all up. Not only did the king wish me to return to London, but he sent me back there as his confidential commissioner, to answer, in my own name, for these libels being entirely destroyed by fire."

The manuscript, and the three thousand copies of the " Memoirs of Madame du Barry," were indeed burnt in the environs of London, in a plaster furnace; but it could hardly be imagined what this interesting operation cost. To purchase the silence of Morande, and preserve the reputation of Madame du Barry from the attacks of his pen, the French Government gave this adventurer 20,000 francs in ready money, besides an annuity of 4000 francs. It has been erroneously asserted that this pension of 4000 francs was suppressed during the following reign. It was not merely a pension, it was an annuity duly secured. The pamphleteer had taken his precautions, and his annuity was therefore not suppressed. However, on his application, Louis XVI.'s ministry bought half of this annuity back from him for a fresh sum of 20,000 francs.* It

* The error we have just pointed out occurs in "Michaud's Biographie Universelle," in the article devoted to Morande. This article contains several other errors; it contains one statement especially, to the effect that, after the death of Louis XV. Morande had the audacity to publish the work whose suppression had been purchased from him so dearly. This is not accurate. Morande was then dependent upon Beaumarchais, who would not have permitted such a breach of faith. The anonymous work, entitled "Anecdotes sur la Comtesse de Barry," which appeared in 1776, is not by Morande; he is even very much abused in this book, which Barbier's "Dictionnaire des ouvrages Anonymes" attributes to Mairobert.

must be confessed that Madame du Barry's honour was estimated very much above its value. For the rest, this Morande had contrived to make himself useful. "He was an audacious poacher," writes Beaumarchais to M. de Sartines; "I have made him an excellent gamekeeper." At a later period, during the American war, he supplied the French Government with information of interest.

As Beaumarchais was publicly reproached by Mirabeau with having been connected with a man of bad repute, in a celebrated attack of which we shall afterwards speak, I determined to obtain a correct idea of the matter, by running through a bundle of letters written by Morande. These letters, far from injuring Beaumarchais, are rather a testimony in his favour. Morande's tone is not one of intimacy and familiarity, but of respect. It can be seen that he dreads his correspondent's bad opinion, and that he wishes to alter his conduct in order to gain Beaumarchais' esteem. "You judge of me," he writes, "from ancient data, which are no longer correct or just. I cannot efface my faults, nor perhaps cause them to be forgotten; but I can prove by succumbing, after making all the efforts it was possible for a man to make, that I am no longer the person whom you perhaps see in me. My heart suffers more from your opinion, than from the evils by which I am overwhelmed." It is true that these protestations are often accompanied by requests

for money, and are not always followed up by perform-
ances.   Morande had married an estimable woman,
belonging to a respectable English family; he made
her sufficiently unhappy, and Beaumarchais, whose
tone is always severe, gives him plenty of reprimands
and good advice.   This good advice at last bore its
fruits, for Morande, as he got older, got better. After
returning to France in 1790, he passed honourably
through the first storms of the Revolution, and withdrew after the 10th of August to his native place,
Arnay-le-Duc, where he exercised for some time,
under the Directory, the functions of justice of the
peace, and died there, leaving a better reputation
than that which his career as a writer of libels had
obtained for him.*

* It is always with regret that I speak of persons to whose conduct I am obliged to apply harsh terms, even when these persons have
long ceased to live. Although each one of us is responsible for his
own faults alone, I can understand how painful it must be for children,
or grand-children, who are often honourable, as far as they themselves are concerned, to see the memory of a father, or ancestor, subjected to severe criticism. If Morande's life had not been mixed up,
in the circumstance I have just spoken of, with that of Beaumarchais;
or if, again, Morande had only been a private individual, up to that
time unknown to the public; and if there had been some injurious
revelation to make in reference to him, I should not have felt myself
bound to undertake the task, and to rescue his name from obscurity;
but this is not the case. The name of Morande is the name of one of
the most noted and decried libel-writers of the eighteenth century.
Amongst all the published documents of this epoch, perhaps not one
could be quoted in which his name figures without being accom-

The unpublished letter of Beaumarchais, which was written immediately after the destruction of the " Memoirs of Madame du Barry," acquaints us with the result of his negotiation with Morande, and at

panied by a degrading epithet. All the biographical collections published in the eighteenth century, represent Morande under the same aspect. Michaud's " Biographie Universelle," for instance, contains an article on him by a native of Burgundy, who was his compatriot, M. Foisset, in which the author of the " Journalist in Armour " is the object of the gravest imputations. I have, then, only reproduced, with a little softening down, that which has been said many times about Morande, rectifying some errors which have been made with regard to him, and stating for the first time that age produced a notable improvement in the man's life. However, one of Morande's grandsons by the female side, after having allowed more severe criticisms than mine to pass without observation, did me the honour, when this work was first published, to display the most indefatigable zeal in trying to obtain from me a kind of rehabilitation for his ancestor. According to him, Morande had nothing to reproach himself with except levities of youth, which had been envenomed and distorted by calumny. I respect family feelings very much, but I cannot sacrifice truth to them. The sale of the "Memoirs of Madame du Barry," which is an undoubted fact, was a piece of extortion of the worst character. Morande, it is true, after often calumniating others, may have also been calumniated in his turn ; but the numerous letters from him which I possess contain confessions which, while they announce a praiseworthy feeling on his part, of repentance as regards the past, and of good resolutions for the future, do not allow me to represent him as a man guilty only of youthful levity. All that I can do, then, while remaining faithful to the first duty of a writer, is to lay a little more stress on the more honest part of Morande's life, which has hitherto been only touched upon very lightly by those who have spoken of him. Morande, through the protection of Beaumarchais himself, had gained a position which

the same time enables us to comprehend his position
with regard to him.

"You have done your best, Sir," he writes to Morande,
"to prove to me that you are returning in good faith to the

was more avowable. During many years he edited the "Courrier de
l'Europe," in England, which I have looked over, and which is
generally written with more decency than could be expected from the
author of the "Journalist in Armour."   Subsequently, when he
returned to France, at the commencement of the Revolution, it might
have been thought, from his antecedents, that he would have taken
his place on the stronger side, and "howled with the wolves," that is
to say, the Jacobins.   He did nothing of the kind; he founded, under
the title of the "Patriotic Argus," a journal with which I was not
acquainted, and which his family communicated to me.   In this
journal, published in 1791 and 1792, Morande defends, with a courage
which circumstances render very meritorious, and often with real
talent, the constitutional monarchical party—the party of moderation,
of reason, and of justice; the party for which the noble and unfortunate André Chénier was combating at the same time.   The author
of the "Patriotic Argus" appears full of respect for Louis XVI., at a
period when the best of kings was still the victim of the most
infamous outrages, and full of intrepidity against a redoubtable and
desperate faction, this journal is certainly a testimonial in favour of the
man who edited and signed it.   It is to this attitude that Morande
owed the honour of being arrested after the 10th of August, and of
escaping only by a happy chance, from the massacres of September.*
It is just, then, to take this portion of his life into account ; but if it
should mitigate the blame which the very serious errors of his youth
deserve, it ought not to do away with it altogether. The man to whom
Beaumarchais could write, in a friendly manner, and without offending
him : "You have become an honourable citizen, descend no more from

* It is also an error, in the "Biographie Universelle," to make Morande
perish in the September massacres ; he did not die until long afterwards, and
he survived Beaumarchais.

sentiments and conduct of an honest Frenchman, from which your own heart has reproached you, long before myself with having wandered ; it is owing to the conviction that you intend to persist in these praiseworthy resolutions, that I take a pleasure in corresponding with you. What a difference in our destinies !—By chance I am selected for stopping the publication of a libellous work; I work day and night during six weeks; I travel nearly 700 leagues ;* I spend nearly 500 louis to prevent evils without number. You gain 100,000 francs, and your peace of mind, by the transaction, while I do not even know whether I shall be reimbursed for my travelling expenses."

The operation had indeed been more profitable to the libeller than to Louis XV.'s agent. While the former received 20,000 francs, and a deed giving him an annuity of 4000 francs, Beaumarchais on returning to Versailles to receive the thanks of the old king, and preparing to remind him of his promises, found him dying. Some days afterwards Louis XV. was dead. "I reflect with astonishment," he writes at this date, "on the strange fate which pursues me. If the king had lived in health for eight days longer, I should have regained my civil rights, of which I have been deprived by injustice. I had his royal word for

the height which you have reached," must have been a man whose conscience told him incontestably, that he had not always been an honourable citizen.

* In these 700 leagues several journies from Paris to London, and from London to Paris are reckoned, besides a journey to Holland to stop an edition of Morande's work.

it, and the unjust aversion with which he had been inspired towards me would have changed to benevolence, and even to predilection." The new king caring much less than Louis XV. for the reputation of Madame du Barry, might be expected to attach less importance to Beaumarchais' services. However, the manufactory of libels established in London, was not in want of work. Louis XVI. and his young wife had hardly ascended the throne, amid the applause of all France—which was happy at seeing there was at last an end to the scandals of the preceding reign—when a dark tissue of lies and calumnies were already being prepared against them, and above all, against the queen. These anonymous insults, which the conflict of opinions under free governments renders at once more rare and more dangerous, become affairs of state under a *régime* of silence. Discussion being absent, it is naturally replaced by defamation, and the existence of the governing powers is worn out in combining little plans for removing little obstacles, which re-appear and become multiplied incessantly. The commission that Beaumarchais had fulfilled under Louis XV., suggested the idea of employing him again in operations of the same nature. In passing from the direction of the police to the ministry of marine, M. de Sartines had maintained friendly relations with him; he himself in the sad position, for which he was indebted to the Maupeou Parliament felt it necessary not to let himself be forgotten by the new government. There was, moreover, an attraction for him here, which did not exist in the preceding mission. To labour for Louis XV. and Madame du Barry had been an affair of necessity; to serve the interests of a king, who was young, true-hearted, and honourable, to prevent calumny from tarnishing with its impure breath the respect due to a young, beautiful and virtuous queen, was an enterprise which might well inspire Beaumarchais with a praiseworthy and sincere zeal. Accordingly on this occasion he did not wait to be asked; he advanced and offered his services. "All the king wishes to know alone and promptly," he writes to M. de Sartines, "all he wishes to do quickly and secretly himself,—here I am: I have at his service a head, a heart, arms, and no tongue. Before the present time I never wished for a patron: this one pleases me; he is young, he means well. Europe honours him, and the French adore him. Let each one in his sphere aid this young prince to deserve the admiration of the entire world, of which he has already the esteem."

As Beaumarchais' zeal could not, on account of his sentence, be made use of officially, it was still in the capacity of secret agent that Louis XVI.'s government sent him to London in June 1774. It was again necessary to stop the publication of a libel which was considered dangerous. This one was called "Notice to the Spanish Branch on its right to the Throne of France in default of Heirs." Under the appearance of a political dissertation the pamphlet was specially directed against the queen Marie-Antoniette; its author was not known, it was only known that its publication was intrusted to an Italian Jew, named William Angelucci, who in London bore the name of William Hatkinson, who used a number of precautions to preserve his incognito, and who had at his disposition enough money to get two large editions of his libel printed at the same time, one for London, the other for Amsterdam.

On accepting this second mission, which was to be so fertile in adventures, Beaumarchais, whether he thought it necessary to increase somewhat the importance of his part, or considered this proof of confidence was necessary to its success, had asked for an order written in the king's own hand. The king, on his side, fearing doubtless that the negotiator might make too free a use of his name, had refused it; Beaumarchais went off, nevertheless: but he was tenacious, skilful, and little accustomed to give up what he wished for; and it is rather curious to observe how, in a series of letters to M. de Sartines, he came back to the charge incessantly, in a thousand different ways, until he at last obtained what had been in the first instance refused. "He can do nothing

without this order written in the king's hand. Lord
Rochford, formerly the English Ambassador at
Madrid, with whom he is intimate, and who might
serve him usefully as minister at London, will not
put himself forward if he is not certain that a personal service has to be rendered to the king. How
can it be feared that he will compromise the king's
name? This sacred name," he says, " will be looked
upon by me as the Israelites regarded the supreme
name of Jehovah, the syllables of which they dared
not pronounce except in cases of supreme necessity. . . . . . The presence of the king, it is said, is
worth fifty thousand men to the army : who knows
how much his name may spare me in guineas?"
After having developed his argument in the most
varied manner, Beaumarchais, seeing that it does not
succeed, undertakes to prove to M. de Sartines that
unless he obtains what he desires his mission fails;
and that if it fails M. de Sartines himself is lost :—

"If the work sees the day," he writes, "the queen,
justly indignant, will soon know that it might have been
suppressed, and that you and myself had undertaken to
suppress it. I am as yet nothing, and cannot fall from very
high; but you! Do you know any woman who forgives an
insult? 'They could stop,' she would say, 'the work which
calumniated the late king and his mistress; by what odious
predilection have they allowed this one to circulate?' Will
she examine whether the intrigue which affects her is not
better combined than the other, and whether precautions

have not been better taken by those who have watched. She
will only see you and me. For want of knowing whom to
attack, she will let all her anger fall upon us; and its least
effect will be, to insinuate to the king that you are nothing
but an unskilful minister, of few resources, and scarcely fitted
for great things. As for me, I shall perhaps be looked upon
as a man who has been bought over by the adversary, whoever he may be; they will not even do me the favour
to think that I am only a fool, they will think I am a
rogue. Then let us be prepared, you to see your credit
weakened, fall and perish, and I to become what it may
please the fate which pursues me."

In the same letter, Beaumarchais indicates a somewhat ingenious process for the use of negotiators of
all kinds, who might happen to blush :—

" I have seen Lord Rochford," he writes, " and found him
as friendly as ever; but when I explained this affair to him,
he remained as cold as ice. I tried him in everyway; I ap-
pealed to his friendship; claimed his confidence; excited his
amour propre, by giving him to hope that he would be making himself agreeable to our king; but I could tell by the
nature of his answers, that he looked upon my commission as
a police affair and one of espionage, in a word, as an underhand proceeding; and as the idea which he had formed suddenly filled my heart with humiliation and mortification,
I blushed like a man who had degraded himself by a vile
commission. I must add, that, feeling myself blush, I stooped
as if my buckle had hurt my foot, so that on rising my red-
ness could pass for the natural effect of a rush of blood to the
head, in consequence of the position I had taken. This lord
is not very cunning; in any case he will not serve me, and I
run the greatest risk of not succeeding. I have already ex-

plained the fatal consequences of such a thing. This may be the speck of a storm, which will burst in all its violence over your head and mine. You must do impossibilities to induce the king to send me an order or commission, bearing his signature in terms similar to those which I gave in my second extract, and which I will copy at the end of this letter; the task is as delicate as it is now essential for you. So many beggars and scamps have come to London in reference to the last libel, that everything which appears connected with the same object, can only be looked upon here with great contempt. This is the basis of your argument with the king, but give him the details of my visit to the lord. It is certain that this minister—although my friend—cannot be decently required to confide in me for the advantage of my master, if this master makes no difference between the delicate and secret mission with which he honours an honest man, and the order which he issues to a police officer, who undertakes one of his ordinary inquiries."

In this long despatch to M. de Sartines, of which we quote only a small portion, the reader, not to speak of the extreme freedom of Beaumarchais' relations with the minister, will see with what clever persistence he brings everything back to his fixed idea, that of obtaining a written order in the hand of the king. There is, doubtless, some exaggeration in his reasoning; he is a man who wishes his services to be valued, and increases, as much as he can, both the importance of a libel, the danger of displeasing an irritated queen, and the fragile tenure of a minister. There is also something true in this argument, as applicable to governments in which personal questions absorb all others. M. de Sartines no doubt thought, at last, that his ministerial prospects were bound up with Beaumarchais' wishes, for he made the young king copy the form of an order which his correspondent, with wonderful *aplomb*, had composed himself, and which was in the following terms :—

> "M. de Beaumarchais, intrusted with my secret orders, will leave for his destination as soon as he possibly can; the discretion and promptness he may display in their execution, will be the most agreeable proof he can give me of his zeal for my service.
>
> "Louis.
>
> "Marly, July 10, 1774."

I have not found, in the papers which were entrusted to me, the text of this order, written in the king's hand; but it is seen from the letter which follows the one just given, that Beaumarchais at last received it :—

> "The order of my master," he writes to M. de Sartines, "is still in its virginity; that is to say, it has been seen by no one; but if it has not yet served me, in connection with other persons, it has, nevertheless, been of wonderful assistance to myself, in increasing my strength and doubling my courage."

In another despatch Beaumarchais addresses the king himself, in the following terms :—

> "A lover carries round his neck the portrait of his mistress : a miser fastens his keys there; a devotee his reliquary; as

for myself, I have had a gold box made, large, oval, and flat, in the form of a lens, in which I have inclosed your majesty's order, suspending it by a little gold chain to my neck, as the thing which is most necessary for my labours, and most precious to myself."

Once decorated with his gold box round his neck, the negotiator went to work, entered into relations with the Jew Angelucci, and endeavoured to persuade him to destroy a libel, for the publication of which the secret enemies of the queen had offered him everything. He succeeded by a great outlay of eloquence, but also, as usual, by a great outlay of money. For 1400 pounds sterling, (about 35,000 francs,) the Jew abandoned his speculation. The two contracting parties went afterwards to Amsterdam to destroy the Dutch edition also. Beaumarchais made Angelucci agree in writing to the fairest conditions in the world, and, free from all care, gave himself up to the pleasure of visiting Amsterdam in the capacity of a tourist. All at once he heard that the astute child of Israel, of whom he had thought himself sure, had started suddenly and secretly for Nuremberg, taking away with him the money he had given him, and a volume which had escaped his observation, and which was about to be reprinted. Beaumarchais became furious, and prepared to follow him. His letters at this period of his negotiation exhibit a feverish impatience.

"I am like a lion," he writes to M. de Sartines; "I have

no more money, but I have diamonds and jewels ; I am going to sell everything, and, with rage in my heart, I must recommence travelling like a postilion. I do not understand German, the roads I am to take are unknown to me, but I have procured a good map, and I already see that I must go to Nimeguen, to Cleves, to Dusseldorf, to Cologne, to Frankfort, to Mayence, and finally to Nuremberg. I shall travel day and night if I do not drop from fatigue on the road. Woe to the abominable man who forces me to go three or four hundred leagues further, when I thought I was about to repose. If I find him on the road, I shall strip him of his papers and kill him, for the pain and trouble he has caused me."

Such was the state of mind in which Beaumarchais pursued the Jew Angelucci through Germany. He met with him at last near Nuremberg, at the entrance to the forest of Neustadt, trotting along on a little horse, and little suspecting that anything disagreeable was galloping behind him. At the sound of the postchaise Angelucci turned round, and recognising the man he had deceived, rushed into the wood. Beaumarchais jumped from his postchaise and pursued him, pistol in hand. Before long the Jew's horse, impeded by the trees, which became thicker and thicker, was forced to stop. Beaumarchais seized his man by the boot, threw him off his horse, turned his pockets out, and emptied his valise, at the bottom of which he found the copy which had escaped his vigilance. In the meanwhile Angelucci's supplications somewhat softened the ferocious temper we have just seen him exhibit; he not only did not kill him, but even left him a portion of the bank-notes which he had given him. After this operation, he came back through the forest to regain his carriage, when an incident occurred which is already known from a letter published in his works. Just after he had quitted Angelucci, he found himself attacked by two brigands, one of whom, armed with a long knife, asked him for his money or his life. He snapped his pistol at him, but the priming did not take: after being knocked down from behind, he received a blow from a knife, which was aimed full at his breast, and which happily came against the famous gold box containing Louis XVI.'s note; the point slid along the metal, scarred the breast, and went into Beaumarchais' chin. He rose by a desperate effort, tore the knife from the robber—wounding himself in the hand with the blade—knocked him down in his turn, and was about to throttle him; but the second assassin, who had at first run away, returned with his companions, and the scene was about to become fatal to Louis XVI.'s secret agent, when the arrival of his servant and the sound of the postilion's horn put the robbers to flight.*

* In the letter written from Germany to be shown to his friends, and which was published during his lifetime, Beaumarchais only relates the scene of the two robbers; he does not say a word in reference to his secret mission to the Jew Angelucci.

All this narrative is so romantic, that we should hesitate about believing it, if the papers relating to this affair did not contain a *procès-verbal*, drawn up by the burgomaster of Nuremberg, at the command of Maria-Theresa, after another incident not less extraordinary, which we shall presently relate. In this *procès-verbal*, dated September 7, 1774, the citizen Conrad Gruber, keeping the inn of the Red Cock at Nuremberg, sets forth how M. de Ronac, that is to say, Beaumarchais, arrived at his house, wounded in the face and hand, on the evening of the 14th of August, after the scene in the wood; and he adds a detail which quite confirms the feverish state which we thought we could perceive in Beaumarchais' own letters. He declares that M. de Ronac had been very restless, that he had risen very early in the morning, and had run all over the house, so that, to judge from all his conduct, his mind appeared to be wandering a little.

Such a complication of incidents might well have produced on Beaumarchais' brain the excitement which this worthy Conrad Gruber mistook for mental alienation; but the traveller was not yet at the end of his adventures, and the last one was to surpass all the others in the extraordinary nature of its incidents.

Fearing that, after his departure from Nuremberg, the Jew Angelucci would go there with some other copy of the libel, and thinking it would be more ad-.

vantageous to get him arrested and conducted to France, Beaumarchais determined to reach Vienna, to solicit an audience from Maria-Theresa, and to beg the empress to grant an order for the man's extradition. As the sufferings occasioned by his wounds rendered a land journey too painful, he reached the Danube, hired a boat, embarked, and arrived at Vienna. Here we will let him speak for himself; the details which follow, and which have remained completely unknown until now, are so curious, and narrated with so much vividness, that the extract will perhaps not appear too long. We borrow it from a voluminous and unpublished document addressed by Beaumarchais to Louis XVI., after his return to France, and bearing the date of the 15th of October, 1774:—

"My first thought at Vienna," writes Beaumarchais, "was to prepare a letter for the empress. Fearing that the letter might not be seen by her alone, I abstained from explaining my motive in soliciting an audience. I endeavoured simply to excite her curiosity. As I could obtain no access to her, I went to the Baron de Neny, her secretary, who, on my refusing to tell him what I wanted, took me apparently for some Irish officer, or some wounded adventurer, who wished to extort a few ducats from her Majesty's pity He received me as badly as possible; refused to take charge of my letter unless I told him my secret, and would, in short, have shown me the door; but assuming in my turn a tone as haughty as his, I assured him that I held him responsible towards the empress for all the evil his refusal might do to this most im-

portant transaction, unless he instantly undertook to convey
my letter to his sovereign. More astonished at my tone,
than he had been at my appearance, he took my letter reluc-
tantly, and told me I must not hope from that that the empress would consent to see me. 'That, Sir, need not distress
you; if the empress refuses me an audience, you and myself
will have done our duty; the rest is a matter of fortune.'

"The next day the empress admitted me to an interview
with the Count de Seilern, President of the Council at Vienna;
who, on my simply setting forth that I was entrusted with a
mission from the King of France, which I wished to explain
personally to the empress, proposed to conduct me immediately to Schœnbrunn, where her Majesty was. I went there,
although my journey of the previous evening had much
increased my sufferings.

"I first showed the empress your Majesty's order, Sire, the
writing of which, as she told me, she at once recognised;
adding, that I could speak freely before the Count de Seilern,
from whom her Majesty assured me she had no secrets, and
by whose counsels she had always profited.

"'Madame,' I said to her, 'it is less a question of a state-
interest, properly so called, than of the efforts which dark in-
triguers are making in France, to destroy the happiness of
the queen by disturbing the king's peace of mind.' I then
gave her the particulars which have just been read.* At each
incident, joining her hands in surprise, the empress repeated:
'But, Sir, where did you acquire so ardent a zeal for the interests of my son-in-law, and above all, of my daughter?'
'Madame, I was one of the most unfortunate men in France
towards the close of the last reign. The queen, in those
dreadful times, did not disdain to show some sympathy for all
the horrors which were accumulating upon me. In serv-

---

* That is to say, the account of all his operations, of which we
have given an abstract, until his arrival at Vienna.

ing her now, without even a hope that she will ever know of it, I am only acquitting an immense debt; the greater the difficulty of my enterprise, the more eager I am for its success.' The queen deigned one day to say aloud, that I showed too much courage and *esprit* in my defence, to have committed the wrongs which were imputed to me. 'What would she say now, Madame, if, in an affair which equally interests her and the king, she were to see me fail in that courage and in that behaviour which she calls "*esprit?*" She would conclude from it, that I have been wanting in zeal. "This man," she would say, "managed in eight days to destroy a libel which slandered the late king and his mistress, when the ministers of England and France had been making vain efforts, during eighteen months, to prevent its appearance. At the present time, entrusted with a like mission, he fails to succeed in it; either he is a traitor, or he is a fool, and in either case is equally unworthy of the confidence which has been placed in him." 'Such, Madame, are the high motives which have made me brave every danger, despise every suffering, and surmount every obstacle.'

"'But, Sir, what necessity was there for you to change your name?'

"'Madame, I am unfortunately only too well known under my own, throughout the whole of literary Europe, and my printed defence in my last affair has so excited every mind in my favour, that wherever I appear under the name of Beaumarchais, whether I excite an interest which proceeds from friendship or from compassion, or only from curiosity, I am visited, invited, surrounded, and am no longer free to work so secretly as so delicate a commission as mine requires; that is why I have begged the king to allow me to travel under the name of Ronac, in which my passport is made out.'

"The empress appeared to have the greatest curiosity to read the work whose destruction had caused me so much trouble. She read it immediately after our explanation. Her Majesty had the kindness to enter with me into the minutest details upon the subject. She was also kind enough to listen to me a long time. I remained more than three hours and a half with her, and begged her several times, with the most earnest entreaties, not to lose a moment in sending to Nuremberg. 'But would this man have dared to show himself there, knowing that you were going there yourself?' said the empress. 'Madame, by way of giving him a fresh inducement to go there, I deceived him, by telling him that I was about to retrace my steps and to return immediately to France. Besides, he either is, or is not there. In the former case, by having him taken back to France, your Majesty will render an essential service to the king and queen ; in the latter there will, at most, be only a step lost, in addition to one which I beg your Majesty to have executed secretly by searching for some time in all the printing offices of Nuremberg, so as to make sure that this infamous work is not being reprinted there; for with the precautions I have taken elsewhere, I can answer for England and Holland.'

" The empress carried her kindness so far as to thank me for the ardent and thoughtful zeal which I exhibited. She begged me to leave her the pamphlet until the next day, giving me her sacred word that she would send it back to me by M. de Seilern. 'Go to bed,' she said to me with infinite grace, 'and get bled without delay.* It ought never to be forgotten, either here or in France, how much zeal you have shown on this occasion for the interests of your master and mistress.'

"I only enter, Sire, into all these details, in order to

---

* These words of the empress—" Get bled without delay," might well be the result of a similar impression to that of the inn-keeper Conrad Gruber.

make their contrast with the conduct which was soon to be adopted towards me more strongly felt. I returned to Vienna, my head still heated by this conference. I cast upon paper a multitude of reflections which appeared to me to have much importance relatively to the object in question. Count de Seilern undertook to show them to her. In the meanwhile, my book was not returned to me, and the same day, at nine in the evening, I saw eight grenadiers with fixed bayonets, and two officers with drawn swords, enter my room, with an imperial secretary, bearing a message from Count de Seilern, in which he invited me to allow myself to be arrested, reserving to himself, he said 'to explain to me, orally, his reasons for this conduct, which I should certainly approve.' 'No resistance,' said the bearer of the orders.

"'Sir,' replied I, calmly, 'I offer resistance sometimes to thieves; but never to emperors.'

"Seals were placed on all my papers; I asked permission to write to the empress, which was refused me. All my property was taken from me, my knife, my scissors, even my buckles, and this numerous guard was left in my room, where it remained thirty-one days, or 44,640 minutes; for while the hours pass so rapidly to the happy that they can scarcely perceive that they succeed one another, the unhappy mince the hours of grief into minutes and seconds, each of which, taken separately, appears very long to them.* During the whole of this time, one of the grenadiers, with his bayonet fixed, kept his eyes upon me, whether I was awake or asleep.

"Judge of my surprise, my anger! To think of my health during this frightful period, was impossible. The person who had arrested me, came to see me the following day to tranquillise me. 'Sir,' I said to him, 'there is no rest for me until I have written to the empress. What happens to me is

* A souvenir of watch-making, very well adapted to the situation.

inconceivable. Let me have pens and paper, or prepare to
chain me up before long, for this is enough to drive me
mad.'

"At last I was allowed to write; M. de Sartines has all my
letters, which were sent to him; let them be read, it will be
seen what was the nature of the grief which was destroying
me. Nothing of a personal nature affected me; all my despair arose from the horrible sin which was being committed
at Vienna against the interests of your Majesty, by keeping
me a prisoner there. 'Let me be fettered in my carriage,' I
said, 'and taken back to France. I do not listen to the dic-
tates of pride, when duty becomes so pressing. Either I am
M. de Beaumarchais, or I am a scoundrel, who is assuming
his name and his mission. In either case, it is against all
good diplomacy to make me lose a month at Vienna. If I
am a knave, by sending me back to France, my punishment
will be only hastened: but if I am Beaumarchais, about
which it is impossible there can be any doubt, after what has
taken place, if people had been paid to injure the interests of
the king, my master, they could not do anything worse than
arrest me at Vienna, at a time when I could be of use elsewhere.' No answer. I was left eight entire days in this
killing distress. At last an imperial councillor was sent
to interrogate me. 'I protest, Sir,' I said to him, 'against
the violence which is done to me here, to the contempt of all
justice; I come to invoke maternal solicitude, and find myself overwhelmed beneath the weight of imperial authority.'
He proposed I should write what I wanted, offering to be
the bearer of it. I showed in my letter the injury which had
been done to the interests of the king by keeping me with
my arms crossed at Vienna. I wrote to M. de Sartines; I
begged him at least to send off a courier by diligence. I renewed my prayers on the subject of Nuremberg. No answer.
They left me a prisoner an entire month without deigning to
set my mind at rest on any subject. Then, collecting all my

philosophy, and yielding to the fatality of so disastrous a star, I devoted myself at length to taking care of my health. I had myself bled, drugged, and purged. They had treated me like a suspicious character in arresting me; like a lunatic in taking away my razors, knives, scissors, &c.; like a fool in refusing me pen and ink; and it was in the midst of all these evils, disquietude, and annoyance, that I waited for M. de Sartines' letter.

"On giving it me, the thirty-first day of my detention, they said to me: 'You are free, Sir, to remain or to go away, according to your desire or your health.' 'If I should die on the road,' I replied, 'I would not remain a quarter of an hour longer at Vienna.' I was presented with a thousand ducats on the part of the empress. I refused them with pride, but with firmness. 'You have no other money to start with,' they said to me; 'all your property is in France.' 'I will give my bill, then, in return, for what I cannot avoid borrowing for my journey.' 'Sir, an empress does not lend money.' 'And I accept no favours except from my master; and he is sufficiently noble to reward me, if I have served him well; but I will receive nothing; I will, above all, receive no money from a foreign power by which I have been so odiously treated.' 'Sir, the empress will consider you are taking a great liberty with her in venturing to refuse.' 'Sir, the only liberty which a man who is very respectful, but who has also been cruelly insulted, cannot be prevented from taking, is that of refusing a favour. For the rest, the king my master will decide whether I have been wrong in pursuing this conduct; but until his decision, I cannot, and will not adopt any other.'

"The same evening I started from Vienna, and, travelling day and night without rest, I arrived at Paris the ninth day of my journey, hoping that some light would there be thrown on so incredible an adventure as that of my imprisonment at Vienna. The only thing M. de Sartines said to me on the subject was, that the empress had taken me for an adventurer; but, I had shown her an order in the handwriting of your Majesty, I had entered into details, which in my opinion could have left her no doubt respecting me. In consideration of this, I venture to hope, Sire, that your Majesty will not disapprove of my persistence in refusing the money of the empress, and will permit me to send it back to her. I might have looked upon it as a sort of flattering compensation for the error which had been made with respect to me, if I had received a kind message from the empress, or her portrait, or any similar mark of honour, with which I could have met the reproach which is made to me everywhere, of having been arrested at Vienna as a suspicious character; but money, Sire! it is the climax of humiliation for me, and I do not think that I deserved it, for the reward of the activity, zeal, and courage with which I fulfilled my most hazardous commission to the best of my ability.

"I await your Majesty's orders.

"CARON DE BEAUMARCHAIS."

Thus was verified, at the expense of Beaumarchais, the justness of Talleyrand's maxim, "Above all, gentlemen, no zeal." By putting himself to the most outrageous trouble for a trifle, he got a month's imprisonment, and when he complained to M. de Sartines the latter replied to him, "What can be done? the empress took you for an adventurer." There is, it appears to me, much candour in the conduct of the negotiator, who cannot be made to understand that the gold box hanging from his neck, his royal letter, his feverish ardour, his undue consumption of post-horses, his change of name, his attempted assassination, and his robbers—all on account of a worthless pamphlet—formed a sufficiently heterogeneous combination to inspire Maria-Theresa with some distrust, and that what in his own opinion should have rendered him interesting, only served to make him suspected of madness or knavery. It appears, however, that to console him for the thousand ducats, which went so much to his heart, a diamond was sent to him in exchange, with an authorisation to wear it from the empress.

One word now on the payment of expenses in this "important affair." Beaumarchais, whose principal object at the time was to induce the king to facilitate his rehabilitation before the Parliament, gave his services gratis; but post-horses cost a great deal of money, and since the month of March, reckoning the journeys relating to the affair of Morande, the expenses of which were not yet paid, he had travelled 1800 leagues, going and returning, in the king's service. The total of the expenses, including the purchase of the Angelucci libel, and the cost of living in different towns, mounted up to 2783 guineas, that is to say, more than 72,000 francs; so that, if we also reckon the 100,000 francs given to Morande, 172,000 francs were spent, and the activity of an intelligent man was employed during six months, and all this to procure the destruction of two rhapsodies, which

were not worth seventy-two *deniers*. Singular
means of stopping the production of libels, and
singular employment of the public wealth !

In the meanwhile, by displaying much activity in
matters of little importance, Beaumarchais gained
ground. He was in continued correspondence with
M. de Sartines, to whom he transmitted, with a mixture of good sense and jovial familiarity, his observations and views on all the political incidents of the
day ; he went and came without ceasing from Paris
to London, in order to look after the libels, and
already followed with as much attention the quarrel
of the English colonies of America with the mother
country. He was soon had recourse to in another
affair of a still more extraordinary kind than the two
former ones. Hitherto, we have only seen him occupied in tracing out, pursuing, and purchasing the
silence of vulgar libellers ; the French government
was about to bring him into conflict with a person as
celebrated as himself, as keen, almost as witty, and
whose life was not less extraordinary.

CHAPTER XV.

THE success of a mystification is no rare thing in the
annals of mankind; but, of all the mystifications in
history, one of the most strange and most ridiculous
is, beyond contradiction, that which was connected
with the Chevalier d'Eon, who, until the age of
forty-three was looked upon everywhere as a man,
who, in his capacity of man, became successively an
advocate in the Parliament of Paris, censor of belles-
lettres, diplomatic agent, chevalier of Saint Louis,
captain of dragoons, secretary of legation, and who
finally filled for several months the functions of
minister plenipotentiary from the court of France,
at London. After a violent and scandalous quarrel
with the ambassador, Count de Guerchy, whose
post he occupied temporarily, he was dismissed, and
officially recalled by Louis XV., but secretly maintained by him at London, with a pension of 12,000

livres. Soon afterwards, towards 1771, doubts,
springing from an unknown source, engendered in
an unknown manner, were raised about the sex of
this captain of dragoons, and, in the English style,
enormous bets were made to depend on the question.
The Chevalier d'Eon, who might easily have settled
all doubts about the matter, allowed them to increase
and be spread abroad. The betting fever grew twice
as strong, and the opinion that the chevalier was
a woman was not long becoming general. A short
time afterwards, in 1775, Beaumarchais, to whom he
had declared that he was a woman, was sent to order
him, in the name of the king, Louis XVI., to make
his declaration public, and to assume the habits of
his sex. He signed the required declaration, and after
hesitating a little longer as to the change of costume,
resigned himself to it at last, and at fifty years of age
quitted his dragoon's uniform for a petticoat and a
coiffe, and in 1777 appeared at Versailles in this attire, which he wore until his death. A book was
written with his co-operation, under the title of
"Military, Political, and Private Life of Mademoiselle d'Eon," a splendid romance, in which it is told
how his parents baptized him as a boy, although he
was a girl, in order to preserve an estate which his
family was to lose in default of male heirs. The
chevalier, on his side, wrote and published numerous
papers, in which he appeared as a female knight, and

congratulated himself on having been able, in the midst of the tumults of camps, sieges, and battles, "to preserve," in his own words, "that flower of purity intact, pledge so precious and so fragile, alas! of our morals and our faith." He was compared to Minerva and Joan of Arc; Dorat addressed complimentary epistles to this old heroine, the glory of her sex. Writers of the greatest weight, and who might be considered the best informed, were taken in like all the others; and the grave author of the " History of French Diplomacy," M. de Flassan, published the following passage on the subject of the chevalier:—

"It cannot be denied," said M. de Flassan, "that she (the Chevalier d'Eon), presented a species of phenomenon. Nature was deceived in giving her a sex so much in contradiction with her haughty and decided character. *Her mania for playing the part of a man*, and for *deceiving all observers*, rendered· her sometimes ill-tempered, and she treated M. de Guerchy with an impertinence which was inexcusable towards the king's minister. For the rest, she deserved esteem and respect for the constancy with which she concealed her sex from so much piercing scrutiny. The brilliant part which this woman played, in missions of a delicate nature, and in the midst of so many adverse circumstances, proves in particular, that she was more fitted for politics, by her wit and information, than many men who have run the same career."[*]

[*] "Histoire générale et raisonnée de la diplomatie Française," vol. v., p. 454, first edition, 1809.

M. de Flassan wrote the lines we have just quoted in 1809, a year before the death of the Chevalier d'Eon. A year afterwards, 1810, the Chevalier d'Eon died at London, and on the body being examined, it was shown and established in the most authentic manner, that this pretended *chevalière*, whom the historian of "French Diplomacy" reproaches with having a "mania for playing the part of a man, and deceiving all observers," that this pretended *chevalière* was a perfectly formed chevalier.*

What is the meaning of this grotesque mystification, and how is its success to be explained? What motive could induce a man of distinguished rank, a man of wit, an intrepid officer, a secretary of legation, a chevalier of Saint Louis, to make himself pass for a woman during more than thirty years? Was the part forced upon him? If it was forced upon him, how and why could a government require a captain of dragoons, forty-seven years of age, to adopt so ridiculous a disguise? and how could this dragoon of forty-seven years of age, who shaved every morning

---

* This clearly results from the following certificate:—"I certify by the present, that I have examined and dissected the body of the Chevalier d'Eon, in presence of Mr. Adair, of Mr. Wilson, and Father Elysée; and that I found the male organs of generation perfectly formed in every respect. May 23, 1810.—Thos. Copeland, surgeon." To this testimony are adjoined the signatures of a large number of well-known persons, who place the sex of the Chevalier d'Eon beyond all doubt.

like all dragoons,* who, in Beaumarchais' own words
"drank smoked and swore like a German postilion,"
deceive so many persons, beginning with Beaumarchais himself? For the latter, as will be seen, always
believed very sincerely that the dragoon was a woman,
and in love with him, Beaumarchais! How, in fine,
and why, did this masquerade problem become a
sort of question of state, give rise to a host of negotiations, make kings and ministers act, speak, and
write, make couriers travel, and cause, as is always
the case, a great deal of money to be spent? These
different questions, which prove how far Montaigne
was right when he said: "The greater part of our
vocations are farcical,"—these different questions are
far from being made clear.

The most accredited version of the Chevalier
d'Eon's story is the following: Having in his youth
the appearance of a woman, he had been sent by
Louis XV. in feminine disguise to the court of St.
Petersburg. He had got introduced to the Empress
Elizabeth in the capacity of *lectrice,* and had contributed to the establishment of good feeling between

---

* Although d'Eon had but little beard, it is certain he had some;
the shade of the beard can be recognised in a portrait executed in
pastel, which I have seen of him, and which he gave to Beaumarchais.
It is true that his face possesses a certain smoothness, which, joined to
his equally feminine voice, must have contributed to give credibility
to the fable of which he was the subject.

the two courts. Hence would have resulted some
doubts as to his sex. These doubts, after disappear-
ing in the midst of an entirely masculine career, had
been revived and propagated a long time afterwards
by Louis XV. himself, after the scandal occasioned
by the quarrel between d'Eon and the Count de
Guerchy. Not wishing to be harsh to an agent whom
he had employed with advantage in his secret service,
and wishing, on the other hand, to give satisfaction
to the de Guerchy family, to prevent a duel between
the ambassador's young son, who had sworn to avenge
his father, and d'Eon, who was a redoubted duellist;
wishing, in fine, to put a stop to all the consequences
of this quarrel, the king had been led, by the recollection of d'Eon's disguise during his youth, to order
him to allow the rumour of his being a woman to
gain ground. Louis XVI., adopting the politics of his
predecessor, forced him to declare himself a woman,
and to assume a woman's clothes. "This strange
personage," says Madame Campan, "had long been
soliciting to be allowed to return to France; but it
was necessary to find some means of sparing to the
family he had offended, the kind of insult which it
would discover in his return; he was made to take
the costume of a sex to which everything is pardoned
in France."

Such is the story most generally admitted on the
subject of the Chevalier d'Eon; but it appears quite

inconceivable. How indeed can we account for the fact of a king, wishing to stifle the effects of a quarrel, and being unable to find no means more simple than that of changing one of the adversaries into a woman; and for that of an officer of forty-seven years of age choosing to renounce all manly careers, and wear petticoats during the rest of his life, rather than simply undertake to decline a challenge, by order of the king—or rather than remain in disgrace and exile while preserving his liberty and his sex? How, in fine, can we account for the fact that if the Chevalier d'Eon, is only the resigned victim of the wishes of Louis XV., and afterwards adopted by Louis XVI., that when these two kings were dead, when the French monarchy itself had ceased to exist, when d'Eon, in retirement at London, had no longer any interest, either of money or position, in continuing the disguise imposed upon him, how can we account for the fact that he persisted in preserving it until his death?

All this is very singular, and scarcely comprehensible. A new theory was produced some twenty years since, about the Chevalier d'Eon. The views on which it is founded are also most strange, and we even experience some hesitation in reproducing them; however, as they are developed in a work of two volumes, which are declared to be taken from authentic documents,*

* This work is entitled " Memoirs of the Chevalier d'Eon," pub-

we are obliged to say a few words on the subject. The author of this work affirms that if the famous Chevalier d'Eon consented to pass for a woman, it was not for the sake of the de Guerchy family, but to save the honour of the Queen of England, Sophia Charlotte, wife of George III. He pretends that d'Eon having been surprised by the king, a physician who was a friend of the queen's, and of d'Eon, had declared to the king that d'Eon was a woman. George III. had asked Louis XV. about the matter, who, for the sake of his royal cousin's peace of mind had hastened to assure him that d'Eon was a woman. From this day d'Eon was condemned to change his sex, with the consolation of having given a king to England; for the author of the book in question does not hesitate to tell us that he is convinced this pretended woman was the father of George IV.

This revelation on the subject of a queen who has hitherto always passed for a very virtuous woman, in order to be admissible, ought to be supported by conclusive proofs, which we look for in vain in the work entitled " Memoirs of the Chevalier d'Eon." With the exception of a letter from the Duke d'Aiguillon to the Chevalier, which if authentic,

lished for the first time from papers furnished by his family, and other authentic documents, deposited in the Archives des Affaires Etrangères, by M. Gaillardet, author of the " Tour de Nesle."

might give some force to the hypothesis of the
author, although it does not positively point out the
queen, Sophia Charlotte; all that the book says, at
least as regards the principal question, may be
reduced to very daring assertions, and very arbitrary
inductions, accompanied by tales, pictures, and dia-
logues from imagination, which give the work the
character of a novel, and deprive it of all authority.*

* If we wished to discuss M. Gaillardet's hypothesis, objections to
it would not be wanting. How, for instance, can we account for
the fact that d'Eon, determined to save the Queen of England's
honour by giving out that he was a woman, encouraged by his
silence the bets which were made as to his sex, and allowed them to
go on increasing during four years, from 1771, the date of the scene
related by the author of the "Memoirs," until 1775, when d'Eon
signed the declaration dictated to him by Beaumarchais? How can
we account for the fact that, during these four years King George III.,
who, in the hypothesis in question, would have the greatest interest in
throwing light upon the matter, did not employ any of those means
for doing so, which even a constitutional monarch could easily find in
such a case? In fine, if this hypothesis can be made to explain d'Eon's
persistence in retaining his woman's clothes until his death, it renders
quite inexplicable the fact that the queen made no attempt to prevent
the discovery after the chevalier's decease. This discovery, according
to M. Gaillardet, occasioned the king's third and last attack of in-
sanity. Nothing, however, would have been more easy than to avoid
this misfortune, for d'Eon died in a state approaching indigence; and
since, according to the supposition of M. Gaillardet, he was sufficiently
devoted to the queen to sacrifice his life to her during thirty years,
she might certainly, with very little money, have determined him to
go and die in a distant land, instead of remaining exposed at London
to the examination of the surgeons. There would be many more observations to make in reference to M. Gaillardet's hypothesis; the date

We have no intention here of offering any theory of our own about the Chevalier d'Eon. As this singular personage only figures in an accessory manner in Beaumarchais' life, it will be sufficient to take the situation at the moment when their relations began.

We are in May 1775, the Chevalier d'Eon is in London, where he has been in disgrace and exile, since his quarrel with Count de Guerchy, although he has continued, nevertheless, even after Louis XV.'s death, to draw the secret pension of 12,000 francs, which that king granted him in 1776. The doubts raised about his sex appear to date from 1771. The English bets on the subject had been going on since that time, and d'Eon by his silence kept up the uncertainty of the betters. In any case it was not the question of his sex which interested the French government at this epoch, it was another and a graver question. As secret agent of Louis XV., d'Eon had, during many years, a mysterious correspondence with the king and the few persons charged with the direction of his secret diplomacy, which, as is known, he had organised without the knowledge of his ministers. D'Eon exaggerated as much as possible the importance of these papers, which related to the peace concluded between France

of George IV.'s birth, taken in connection with the date of d'Eon's visit to England, does not at all accord with this hypothesis, which appears to us completely chimerical.

and England in 1768. He circulated among his acquaintances, that if they were printed, they would rekindle the war between the two nations, and that the English opposition had offered him enormous sums to publish them; he was, he said, too good a Frenchman to consent to it; but, in the meanwhile he was in want of money, a great deal of money, because he had a great many debts, and if the cabinet of Versailles wished to regain possession of the papers, it must pay the debts of the present possessor. It was not, moreover, a present d'Eon asked for; the French government was his debtor. Indeed it owed him more money than d'Eon owed himself. The Chevalier sent, in 1774, to M. de Vergennes, Minister of Foreign Affairs, a bill of the most amusing description, from which I only extract the following article, to give an idea of the intrepidity with which this dragoon charged the public treasury.

" In November 1757," writes d'Eon, " the present king of Poland being Envoy Extraordinary of the Republic in Russia, sent to M. d'Eon, Secretary of the French Legation, a note, inclosing a diamond estimated at 6000 livres, in the hope that M. d'Eon would inform him of a very interesting affair, which was then being conducted at St. Petersburg; the latter made it his duty to show the note and the diamond to the Marquis de l'Hospital, Ambassador, and to take back the said diamond to the Count de Poniatowski. M. de l'Hospital, touched by the honourable action of M. d'Eon, wrote about

it to the Cardinal de Bernis, who promised to procure him a
grant of like value from the king for his fidelity; but the
Cardinal de Bernis having been displaced and exiled, M.
d'Eon never received this grant, which he thinks he is entitled
to claim. . . . . 6000 livres."

Is not this a good story of a diamond, refused in
1757, and which is claimed as a debt in an account
of 1774? Let us look at another item.

"The Count de Guerchy," says d'Eon, "prevented the
King of England from making to M. d'Eon, the present of a
thousand gold pieces, which he grants to the minister's
plenipotentiary residing at his court. . . . 24,000 livres."

Again :—

"Not having been in a position from 1763 to 1773 to
attend to his vines in Burgundy, M. d'Eon has not only
lost a thousand crowns income per annum, but also all his
vines, and considers he may put this loss down at half its
real amount. . . . . 15,000 livres.
"Moreover, M. d'Eon, without entering into an account
which he might produce of the immense expenses occasioned
by his residence in London, from 1763 until the present year
1773, both for the maintenance and support of his late cousin
and himself, and for the extraordinary outlays occasioned by
circumstances, thinks he ought to confine himself to claiming
the cost at London, of a simple, decent establishment, in
which a person limits himself to mere necessaries and servants, which he consequently estimates at the moderate sum
of 450 louis, or 10,000 livres tournois per annum, making for
the said ten years . . . . 100,000 livres."

It is to be remarked, that since 1766, d'Eon had
received an annual pension of 1200 louis. The valet

of Regnards " Joueur" presents a list of claims which
is certainly not equal to the above. All the remainder
is in the same style, and the total of the ingenious
chevalier's claims is thus raised to the moderate sum
of 318,477 livres 16 sous. D'Eon requested in addition that his pension of 1200 francs might be converted into a deed of annuity for the same amount.
Two negotiators had been sent to him successively, to
obtain the return of these papers on less exorbitant
conditions ; one of them, M. de Pommereux, captain of
grenadiers, and as such gifted with rare intrepidity,
had been so far as to propose to this captain of dragoons, who passed for a woman, to marry him. D'Eon,
not wishing to give up any of his claims, had been determined to let the negotiation drop, when in May
1775, the chevalier, learning that Beaumarchais was
in London on other business, asked to see him. " We
met," said d'Eon, " owing, no doubt, to a natural
curiosity, on the part of extraordinary animals to see
one another." The chevalier solicited Beaumarchais'
support ; and by way of giving him a proof of his
confidence, confessed to him with tears that he was a
woman, and what is strange is, that Beaumarchais
did not doubt it for an instant. Delighted to oblige
a girl so interesting from her warlike courage, her
diplomatic talents, and her misfortunes, and to bring
a difficult negotiation to an end, he addressed to
Louis XVI., the most touching letters in favour of

d'Eon. " When it is thought," he writes to the king, " that this creature, so much persecuted, is of a sex to which everything is forgiven, the heart becomes moved with pity." "I venture to assure you," he writes elsewhere, " that by treating this astonishing creature with skill and kindness, although soured by twelve years' of misfortunes, she can easily be brought under subjection, and made to give back all the papers relating to the late king on reasonable terms." It will be asked how Beaumarchais, who certainly was not wanting in experience in these sort of matters, could imagine he saw a girl instead of a dragoon of the most masculine description. One thing is certain, that in all Beaumarchais' papers, there is not a single line which does not prove that he was indeed completely deceived as to the sex of the chevalier; and if it could be supposed that in this comedy, the author of " The Barber of Seville" was playing a part, and pretending to take a man for a woman, we should be prevented from entertaining this idea, by the candour with which his intimate friend Gudin, who accompanied him in the visit during which the negotiation with d'Eon was effected, relates, in his unpublished memoirs concerning Beaumarchais, the misfortunes of this interesting woman. "It was at the house of Wilkes,* at dinner,

---

* Wilkes was at this time Lord Mayor of London.

that I met d'Eon for the first time. Struck by
the cross of Saint Louis, I asked Miss Wilkes who
this chevalier was; 'he has,' I said, 'a woman's
voice, and from that, apparently, have arisen all the
stories which have been told about him.' I knew no
more about him at the time; I was still ignorant of
his relations with Beaumarchais. I soon ascertained
them for myself. She confessed to me with tears (it
appears that this was d'Eon's style), that she was
a woman, and showed me her legs, which were
covered with scars from wounds she had received
when, after being thrown from her horse, which had
been killed under her, a squadron passed over her
body, and left her almost dead on the plain.

No one could have been mystified with more
naïveté than Gudin. During the first period of the
negotiation, d'Eon paid the most delicate attention to
Beaumarchais: he called him his "guardian angel,"
he sent him his "complete works" in fourteen volumes, which he recommended to his indulgence, for
this strange being, dragoon, woman, and diplomatist,
was at the same time a scribbler of the most prolific
kind. He characterises himself very well in a letter
to the Duke de Praslin.

"If you wish to know me, M. le Duc, I will tell you frankly
that I am only good for thinking, imagining, questioning, re-
flecting, comparing, reading, writing, for travelling from the
east to the west, from the south to the north, and for fighting

on the plain or in the mountains. If I had lived in the time of Alexander or Don Quixote, I should have been Parmenio or Sancho Panza. If you put me to anything else, I should, without committing any absurdity, consume all the revenue of France in a year, after which I would give you an excellent treatise on economy. If you wish for a proof, look at all I have written in my history of the finances, on the distribution of the public wealth."

Under the effect of the pretended *chevalière's* cajolery, Beaumarchais returned to Versailles, pleaded her cause with warmth, exhausted himself in proving that the papers she had in her hands, and with which he was not acquainted, were of the greatest importance, asked permission to renew the negotiations which had been broken off with her, and obtained it in the following letter from M. de Vergennes, which is important as not being in accordance with the version generally adopted of the views entertained by the French government in regard to the Chevalier d'Eon. The following is M. de Vergennes' unpublished letter to Beaumarchais, of which I have only suppressed some insignificant passages :—

"I have beneath my eyes, Sir, the report you have made to M. de Sartines of your conversation respecting M. d'Eon ; it is of the greatest exactitude. I have in consequence taken the king's orders: his Majesty authorises you to agree to all reasonable security which M. d'Eon may demand, for the regular payment of his pension of 12,000 livres, it being well understood that he is not to derive this annuity from any investment out of France ; the capital which would have to be employed for producing it, is not in my power, and I should meet with the greatest obstacles in procuring it; but it is easy to convert the said pension into a life annuity, to which he could hold the title.

" The question of the payment of debts will occasion more difficulty. M. d'Eon's claims are rather high on this point; he must reduce them, and considerably, for us to make an arrangement. As you must not seem, Sir, to have my mission concerning him, you will have the advantage of making him speak first, and consequently will have a superiority over him. M. d'Eon has a violent temper, but I think he has an honest heart, and I do him sufficient justice to be convinced that he is incapable of treachery.

" It is impossible M. d'Eon should take leave of the king of England; *the revelation of his sex can no longer be permitted; it would be ridiculous for both courts.* The testimonial he wishes to have substituted suggests some difficulties; however, it can be granted provided he be contented with the praise which his zeal, his intelligence, and his fidelity deserve; but we cannot praise either his moderation or his subordination; and in any case, there must be no question of the scenes he had with M. de Guerchy.

" You are enlightened and prudent; you know what men are, and I am not uneasy about your arriving at a good result with M. d'Eon, if it is possible to do so. If the enterprise fails in your hands,* it must be taken for granted that it can never succeed, and we must make up our minds for whatever may be the result. The first sensation might be disagreeable for us; but the consequences would be frightful for M. d'Eon. A very humiliating part is that of an exile, who bears the varnish of treason: contempt is his lot.

" I am very sensible, Sir, of the praise you have kindly

---

* That is to say, the enterprise, the object of which was to obtain the return of the secret correspondence of d'Eon with Louis XV.

awarded to me in your letter to M. de Sartines. I aspire to
deserve it, and receive it as a pledge of your esteem, which
will be always flattering to me. Rely, I beg you, upon mine,
and upon all the sentiments with which I have the honour to
be,

"Your very humble and very obedient servant,

"DE VERGENNES.

"Versailles, June 21, 1775."

This letter from M. de Vergennes, which did much
honour to Beaumarchais, proves that at that time no
one thought of making d'Eon assume a woman's
dress; but it proves at the same time that his feminine dress was considered even then as an established
fact. The only condition required for allowing his
return to France, was the return of his correspondence with Louis XV. It is not until two months
afterwards, in a letter to Beaumarchais, dated August
26, 1775, that M. de Vergennes explains himself on
the subject of the woman's costume in the following
terms :—

"Whatever desire I may have to see, to know, and to
hear M. d'Eon, I will not conceal from you, Sir, one source
of uneasiness by which I am besieged. His enemies are on
the watch, and will not easily forgive all he has said of them.
If he comes here, however well-behaved and circumspect
he may be, they may attribute remarks to him contrary to
the silence imposed upon him by the king; denials and jus-
tifications are always embarrassing and odious to honourable
minds. *If M. d'Eon would disguise himself, all would be
arranged; it is a proposition which he alone can make;* but,

for the sake of his own tranquillity he should avoid, at all events for some years, living in France, and necessarily in Paris. You may make what use you think fit of this observation."

The phrase we have just italicised in the minister's second letter, seems to be in contradiction with the one we have italicised in the first. Did M. de Vergennes mean that d'Eon was a man, and that he was to dress himself up like a woman? If so, how are we to make this accord with what he wrote two months previously about the "revelation" of d'Eon's sex? Moreover, and without saying anything about the strangeness of a minister and a man of serious disposition, bringing forward an idea of this kind as quite a simple thing, if M. de Vergennes' phrase had the meaning which it at first sight appears to have, this phrase, addressed to Beaumarchais, would render the letters of the latter completely unintelligible, for he is perpetually speaking of the Chevalier d'Eon's feminine sex. Let us add finally, that this phrase taken literally would also destroy M. Gaillardet's theory, who, to explain Beaumarchais' error, pretends that d'Eon and the minister made an agreement that the agents commissioned to negociate between them, should be themselves misled as to the chevalier's true sex. These considerations led us to think that M. de Vergennes believed like Beaumarchais that d'Eon was a woman, that the word "dis-

guise" was an improper expression which escaped the minister, who only meant to say, "Although M. d'Eon has always passed for a man, since he is at present recognised as a woman, he ought to dress like one." The form of the letter seems to indicate also, that it was written to support the initiative taken by Beaumarchais with regard to the question of woman's attire. It was Beaumarchais, in fact, who insisted particularly on this point.

"All this," he writes to the minister in a letter dated October 7, 1775, "has given me an opportunity of knowing still better the creature with whom I have to deal, and I still keep to what I said to you before, that the feeling of resentment against the late ministers (those who had dismissed him in 1766) and their friends of the last thirty years, is so strong *in him* * that it would be impossible to place too insurmountable a barrier between the contending parties. Written promises of good behaviour are not sufficient to stop a head, which always becomes inflamed at the mere name of Guerchy; his positive avowal of his sex, and an engagement to appear for the remainder of his life in woman's clothes, are the only safeguards against scandal and misfortune. I have required this authoritatively, and have obtained it."

Here, for the rest, is another autograph letter from M. de Vergennes to Beaumarchais, of a later date than the two I have already quoted, having

---

* The word "him," proves nothing against Beaumarchais' error. It is only the result of his being accustomed to look upon d'Eon as a man.

been written February 10, 1776, and in which the minister, while he first speaks of d'Eon, through habit, as a man, seems to be thoroughly persuaded that the chevalier is a woman.

"Versailles, February 10, 1776.

"I must not let you remain ignorant, Sir, that a very exact copy is being circulated in Paris, of the "safe conduct" which you had to give M. d'Eon, in case he should return to France and which could be of no use to him if he renounced returning to his country, or if he returned to it in the costume of his real sex. You can understand that this document causes great scandal among those who imagine there can be no reason for awarding praise to a person who had been in a certain way proscribed, and it is very difficult to enter into an explanation with all the tatlers and all the censors.

"What interest do you think your Amazon can have had in publishing a document which evidently ought not to have left her hands either by a copy or as an extract? I will not suppose that you neglected to impress this upon your Amazon; I am much afraid she is the dupe of some interested persons, who, by their advice, have wished to put her forward in order to give body to some new intrigue. It would be useless to attempt to impede her in what she pleases to do; but if she does not wish to return, as I presume to be the case, try, Sir, if with dexterity you cannot gain the original of a safe conduct, which can be of no advantage to her if she does not mean to make use of it, and which cannot even serve her any longer, since she has promised not to re-enter the kingdom except in woman's clothes. Do not doubt the sincerity of the sentiments with which, Sir,

"I am your very humble and very obedient servant,

"DE VERGENNES."*

* Let us quote in support of our opinion, another unpublished

Beaumarchais and M. de Vergennes appear to
me, then, to have been equally deceived by d'Eon on
the question of sex; but Beaumarchais got the better
of him on the question of money. The chevalier, it
is remembered, asked the trifle of 318,477 livres for
returning the celebrated correspondence. Beaumarchais, while rejecting these absurd claims, mentions
no figure himself; and in the transaction of the 5th
October, 1775, by virtue of which d'Eon declares
himself a woman, and engages to return all the
papers of Louis XV., the agent of M. de Vergennes
binds himself to deliver to him a deed securing him
1200 livres of annuity, in addition to *larger sums, of
which the amount would be remitted to him,* for the
payment of his debts in England. Each of the two
contracting parties had a loop-hole to escape by.
If the larger sums did not appear sufficiently large to
the chevalier, he intended to keep a portion of the
papers in order to obtain larger sums still; as Beaumarchais, on the other hand, did not intend to pay
all the debts it might please d'Eon to declare, he had
obtained from the king the power of "battling," to
employ his expression, with Mademoiselle d'Eon from

letter, addressed by M. de Vergennes to the Chargé d'Affaires, at
London, dated March 23, 1776:—"I should be very pleased if M. de
Beaumarchais could conclude with the *Amazon d'Eon, not that I wish
for her here,* about which I care very little; but in order to be no
longer obliged to pay attention to an adventure which does not
amuse me nearly so much as the pit."

100 up to 150,000 francs, reserving to himself the right of paying the money by instalments, and increasing or diminishing the sum, according to the confidence this cunning personage might inspire him with.

D'Eon commenced by exhibiting an iron chest, well padlocked, which was deposited with an English admiral, his friend Lord Ferrers, as security, he said, for a debt of 5000*l*. sterling. He declared that this chest contained all the secret correspondence. Here was a difficulty for Beaumarchais; he was not authorised to look at these papers; but if he gave the money without doing so, he might, he says, receive in exchange nothing but washing-bills. After a fresh journey to Paris to obtain permission to make an inventory of the papers, he at last received the authorisation, and on the chest being opened, it was found that Lord Ferrers, the real or pretended creditor, had only received, as security, papers of scarcely any importance. D'Eon confessed then with blushes, that the most important papers had remained concealed beneath the floor of his bed-room. "She conducted me to her house," writes Beaumarchais, "and drew from beneath the flooring five card-board boxes, well sealed, and labelled 'secret papers, to be remitted to the king alone,' which she assured me contained the whole of the correspondence, and the entire mass of the papers which she had in her possession. I commenced by making an inventory, and marking them all, so that

none of them might be taken away; but to make more
sure that the entire mass was there, I ran through
them rapidly, while she was writing the inventory."

It is seen that Beaumarchais was a man of precau-
tion; then only did he pay Lord Ferrers' claim, who
remitted to him in exchange an equal sum in bills
accepted by the Chevalier d'Eon, after which he prepared to start for Versailles with his chest. The chevalier naturally considered *the larger sums* not sufficiently large; but as the transaction of October 5, not
only stipulated for the return of the papers, but also
bound d'Eon to wear woman's clothes, and to remain
silent concerning all his old disputes with the Guerchy
family, Beaumarchais took a high hand with him :—

"I assured this young lady," he writes to M. de Vergennes,
"that if she was good, modest, silent, and behaved herself
well, I would give a good account of her to the king's minister,
even to his Majesty himself, and that I hoped to obtain some
still further advantages for her. I made this promise the
more willingly, from the fact that I had still about 41,000
livres of Tours in my hands, out of which I meant to reward
each act of submission and good behaviour, as if doing so
through the special generosity of the king or yourself,
M. le Comte, and only as gratuities, not as payments. It
was by means of this secret proceeding that I still hoped to
govern and rule this impetuous and cunning creature."

When he arrived at Versailles with his chest,
Beaumarchais was complimented by M. de Vergennes,
who sent him a magnificent certificate, declaring that

his Majesty had been much satisfied with the zeal
he had shown in this matter, and the intelligence
and skill with which he had accomplished the commission his Majesty had intrusted to him.* The
negotiator was beginning to attract the attention of
Louis XVI. The preceding missions had left him in
the shade, this one was putting him in a prominent
position. He was not a man to remain there, and
to neglect his point. Before starting again for
London he addressed to Louis XVI. a series of questions, begging the king to be kind enough to answer
them in the margin, and the king, with his own
hand, replied obediently to Beaumarchais' questions.
The autograph is interesting; the body of the document is written in Beaumarchais' hand, and signed
by him; the answers to each question are traced in
the margin, in a writing which is rather elegant, but
unequal, weak and irresolute, the t's and v's being
scarcely indicated. It is the characteristic writing of
the good, weak, unhappy sovereign, who was destined
seventeen years afterwards to be swallowed up by the
revolution; and in order that the secret agent might
glory at his ease in having been in direct correspondence with Louis XVI., the answers of the
monarch are followed by the annexed attestation,
written and signed in the hand of M. de Vergennes

---

* See the certificate in the Appendix, No. 4.

—*All the answers to the questions are in the king's hand.*" In order to appreciate this document, as a sign of the discordance of all things during this period of French history, it must not be forgotten that at the period at which it was prepared, Beaumarchais was suffering from the effect of a legal condemnation which declared him to have lost all rights of citizenship; and it is in this position that he commences in writing the following dialogue with Louis XVI. :—

"Essential points, which I beg M. le Comte de Vergennes to present for the king's decision, before my departure for London, this 13th Dec., 1775; to be replied to in the margin :—

"Does the king grant to Mademoiselle d'Eon permission to wear the cross of St. Louis on her woman's clothes?

"*Answer of the king*—In the provinces only.

"Does his Majesty approve of the gratuity of 2000 crowns, which I have given to this young lady on her assuming woman's clothes?

"*Answer of the king*—Yes.

"Does his Majesty in this case leave her man's clothes at her entire disposition?

"*Answer of the king.*—She must sell them.

"As these favours are to be dependent upon a certain frame of mind, into which I wish to bring Mademoiselle d'Eon for ever, will his Majesty leave me the power of granting or refusing, according as I may think useful for the good of his service?

"*Answer of the king.*—Yes.

"As the king cannot refuse to give me through his

Minister of Foreign Affairs, an acknowledgment in good form, of all the papers I have brought back to him from England, I have begged the Count de Vergennes to entreat his Majesty to be kind enough to add at the bottom of this acknowledgment, *in his own hand*, a few words of satisfaction as to the manner in which I fulfilled my mission. This reward, the dearest to my heart, may also one day be of the greatest utility to me; if some powerful enemy ever pretended to ask me for an account of my conduct in this affair, with one hand I would show the order of the king, with the other I would present my master's attestation, that I have fulfilled his orders to his satisfaction. All the intermediate operations will then become a deep ditch, which each one will fill up according to his pleasure, without my being obliged to speak, or ever troubling myself about what may be said on the subject.

"*Answer of the king.*—Good."

Here the subject of the dialogue changes. As long as it is only necessary to decide whether d'Eon is to wear the cross of St. Louis on his woman's clothes, and to sell his man's clothes, Louis XVI. gives very clear and very precise answers; but Beaumarchais wishes to lead him further, and we shall see that in some months he will succeed. For the moment, he is too much pressed, and too pressing. He passes without transition from the d'Eon affair to the American affair, and seeks to gain by assault the king's adhesion to plans, with which he has been pursuing him for some time. Louis XVI. maintains reserve, and the tone of his answers changes. The meaning of what follows will be clearly explained when we come to treat of Beaumarchais' influence in the American question ; but, as all this written dialogue is contained in the same letter, we have thought it desirable not to mutilate it, for fear of depriving it of its true aspect. We accordingly continue to quote it.

"As the first person I shall see in England will be my Lord Rochford, and as I have no doubt that this lord will ask me secretly, what answer the king of France gives to the prayer the king of England addressed to him through me, what shall I reply to him on the part of the king ?

"*Answer of the king*—That you received none.

"If this lord, who has certainly preserved much of his intimacy with the king of England, wishes secretly to induce me to see this monarch, shall I consent or not ? This question is not an idle one, and deserves to be well weighed before giving me my orders.

"*Answer of the king*—That may be.

"It having been the design of this minister to admit me into the secrets of a policy especially his own, if he wished now to connect me with other ministers, or if, in whatever manner it might happen, the opportunity should be offered to me, shall I accept or not ?

"*Answer of the king*—It is useless.

"In the case of the affirmative I cannot do without a cypher. Will the Count de Vergennes give me one ?

"*No answer.*

"I have the honour to inform the king that the Count de Guines * has endeavoured to render me an object of suspicion to the English ministers. Shall I be permitted to say a few words to him on the subject, or does his Majesty wish

* The French Ambassador at London.

that, while continuing to serve him, I should appear ignorant of all the dark means which have been employed for injuring me personally, my operations, and consequently the good of his service ?

"*Answer of the king*—He (the ambassador) must remain in ignorance."

The king meant that M. de Guines was not to be informed of what Beaumarchais was doing in London, in reference to the position of the insurgent colonies. What follows is the gravest part of the · letter; and accordingly the king makes no reply to it.

"Finally, I request before starting, a positive answer to my last note; * but if ever a question was important it must be admitted that it is this one. I answer with my head, after mature reflection, for the most glorious success of this operation, during the entire reign of my master, without either his own person, that of his ministers, or his interests being ever in any way injured thereby. Will any one of those who dissuade his Majesty from it, dare to answer in his turn, also with his head, to the king for all the evil which must infallibly come to France, from their causing it to be rejected? In case we should be sufficiently unfortunate for the king to refuse steadily to adopt so simple and wise a plan, I entreat his Majesty, at least, to be permitted to take down the date, in his presence, of the period at which I offered him this admirable resource, so that he may one day render justice to the

* The object of this note, of which we shall speak again, was to determine the king to send secretly through Beaumarchais, assistance in arms and ammunition to the American colonies.

correctness of my views, when all that will remain will be to regret bitterly not having followed them.

"CARON DE BEAUMARCHAIS."

This singular dialogue between Louis XVI. and Beaumarchais seems to represent very well the prudent disposition of the one, and the active disposition of the other. The temerity of the secret agent will soon finish, by gaining the victory over the prudence of the king, and Beaumarchais, who has only put forward the trifling questions about d'Eon, in order to reach the great ones about America, is obliged to start again for London, having only ascertained that d'Eon is to sell his man's clothes. He found the chevalier, who to him is always a *chevalière*, somewhat unfaithful to the promises of modesty and silence which he had made in the transaction of the 5th October. Under the pretext of stopping the bets made about his sex, he called attention to himself in the English journals, with that vain display, which was habitual to him, and as his announcements were composed so as still to leave in mystery a point which should have been considered as settled, they were more fitted to tempt the bettors than to discourage them. Beaumarchais reproached him rather hastily; the chevalier, more hasty still than Beaumarchais, seeing, moreover, that his austere friend kept the king's purse-strings tightly drawn, became quite angry. Hence a rupture, and an interchange of letters in which d'Eon,

after offering Beaumarchais the most masculine insults, endeavoured to take advantage of his fatuity by
suddenly re-assuming the tone of a young lady, and
complaining amorously of the ingratitude of this
perfidious man.

" I confess, Sir," writes this dragoon in woman's clothes ;
" I confess that a woman may sometimes find herself in such
unfortunate situations, that circumstances may oblige her to
profit by services of which she is the first to see the absurdity, because she penetrates the motive.* The greater the
skill and delicacy of the man who wishes to oblige her,
the greater the danger for her; but what souvenirs do these
reflections recal to me! They recal to me that, by a blind
confidence in you and your promises, I discovered to you the
mystery of my sex; that through gratitude I gave you my
portrait, and that through esteem you promised me yours.

" There have been many other engagements between us ;
all that you have advanced beyond that, as to our approaching marriage, according to what I hear from Paris, can only
be regarded by me as mere *persifflage* on your part. If you
have made a serious matter of a simple pledge of friendship

* The most striking thing in d'Eon's letters, written to Beaumarchais, of which I only quote some fragments, is, that while sustaining
as well as possible before him this part of a woman, concealed under
the appearance of a man, he often gives to his phrases an enigmatic
turn, by which he would seem to have wished to establish clearly, for
the period when his fraud would be discovered, that he was duping a
man, as cunning as the author of " The Barber of Seville;" and that
he was duping him, and at the same time laughing in his face, without
the latter perceiving it. Beaumarchais, on his side, was amusing himself at the expense of this *amorous old she-dragoon*, and was becoming
the more confirmed in his error, in proportion to the skilful manner
in which d'Eon simulated the anger of an offended old maid.

and gratitude, your conduct is pitiable. That would be a
true piece of contempt, and a breach of faith, which a woman
of Paris, however much she might be broken-in to fashionable
morals, could not pardon; still less a woman whose virtue is
as uncivilised as mine, and whose disposition is so haughty,
when the good faith and sensibility of her heart are wounded.
Why did I not remember that men are only on the earth to
deceive the credulity of girls and women? . . . . . I only
thought, too, that I was rendering justice to your merit, ad-
miring your talents, your generosity. I loved you, doubtless even then; but the situation was so new to me, that I
was very far from thinking love could arise in the midst of
trouble and grief."

Beaumarchais replied to d'Eon in the grave tone of
a man who has a duty to fulfil, and means to remain
insensible to the reproaches and insinuations of an
angry old maid; and, as he suspects less than ever
that he is being mystified, he writes to M. de
Vergennes :—

"Every one tells me that this mad woman is mad about me.
She thinks I have treated her with contempt, and women
never pardon such an offence. I am far from despising her;
but who the devil would ever have imagined that, to serve the
king properly in this affair, it would have been necessary for
me to become the gallant knight of a captain of dragoons?
This adventure appears to me so absurd, that I have all the
trouble in the world to regain my seriousness, so as to finish
this note properly."

It is certain that if M. de Vergennes had been in
the secret of the chevalier's true sex, which we do not
think he was, he must have had a good laugh in his

turn, but at the expense of Beaumarchais. In any case, as d'Eon was not reasonable and modest, according to the terms of the agreement, and did not assume woman's clothes and return to France, Beaumarchais gave him no more money. D'Eon wrote the most violent and abusive things against him to M. de Vergennes. This "guardian angel" of the first period of the correspondence is only a "conceited fool;" he has "the insolence of a watchmaker's apprentice, who has by accident discovered perpetual movement:" he can only be compared to "*Olivier Ledaim, barber, not of Seville, but of Louis XI.*"

Beaumarchais received these broadsides of insult with the calm of a perfect gentleman. "She is a woman," he replied to M. de Vergennes, "and in such a frightful situation, that I pardon her with all my heart. She is a woman; this explains everything." D'Eon finding that he was considered to have been sufficiently remunerated, pretended to have further papers to publish. Beaumarchais was at first somewhat alarmed about it, but was soon re-assured. It was only a boast of the chevalier's; he had nothing more: he had given things for 120,000 livres,* for

---

* In paying the real or supposed claim of Lord Ferrers, Beaumarchais, who had been authorised to make the best terms he could in paying, had induced d'Eon to allow a discount to the king, which reduced the sum given to 109,000 livres. He had afterwards remitted to d'Eon small sums, which made the total of the money given amount to £4902.

which he had at first wanted 318,000; and Beaumarchais kept him in a certain state of awe, for he retains in his hands the bills bearing his acceptance to Lord Ferrers, and as d'Eon's pension had been converted into a deed of annuity, he could, if necessary, have it seized, provided this pretended young lady persisted in not executing the terms of the treaty. For the rest, knowing the vain disposition of the individual, he recommended M. de Vergennes, if he wished to secure his return to France, to appear not to think of it. Afraid of being forgotten, the chevalier arrived at Versailles of his own accord one fine morning in August, 1777; but he no longer remembered that he had to dress as a woman : he was ordered to assume that costume; he obeyed, and for some time excited much curiosity and interest; when this curiosity had fallen off, he started back to London, and as he had no further connexion with Beaumarchais, we have nothing more to do with him.

In taking leave of the strange affair of the Chevalier d'Eon, we shall be tempted to conclude like Voltaire, who wrote the following lines in reference to the subject in 1777:—"The whole of this adventure confounds me; I can conceive neither d'Eon, nor the ministry of his time, nor the actions of Louis XV., nor those of the present day; I under-

Throughout this affair Beaumarchais appears more economical with the king's money than in the two preceding ones.

stand nothing in this world." There is indeed something incomprehensible about a world in which such masquerades can be made important questions. We will however say, looking at the enigma as it existed under Louis XVI., what seems to us most probable, according to the documents beneath our eyes. Contrary to the most general opinion, it appears to us very probable that Louis XVI. and M. de Vergennes, in forcing d'Eon to wear woman's clothes, thought him really a woman. The serious disposition of the king and of the minister scarcely allows us to suppose that they could have thus lent themselves to so ridiculous and unbecoming a comedy, in which Beaumarchais alone played the part of dupe.* But as this pretended revelation furnished a sufficiently convenient means of stifling all the consequences of the former quarrels of the chevalier with the Guerchy family and their friends, they both hastened to adopt it as a settled thing, without caring much to verify its truth. As for d'Eon, it is evident that from the day when, I do not know by what cause, the doubts which the disguise of his youth had given rise to, appeared again in his more mature age,

---

* Independently of the letters already quoted, several other letters of M. de Vergennes confirm me in this opinion. As for Beaumarchais, the mystification which d'Eon subjects him to, is seen in all his correspondence. See also, in reference to this subject, an unpublished letter from Beaumarchais to d'Eon, in the Appendix, No. 5.

he first of all repelled them, then encouraged them,
and corroborated them the more successfully by ap-
pearing to let the secret of his being, as he pretended,
a woman, be extorted from him with much trouble.
Without attending to the completely romantic hypothesis of M. Gaillardet,* d'Eon appears to us to have
been induced to play this comedy by two motives,
not very lofty in themselves: first of all, the hope of
obtaining from the French government more money
as an interesting *amazon*; next and above all, vanity,
a want to get spoken of at any price, which is the
most marked trait in his character. In an unpublished letter of his to a friend, we read the following
lines: "I am a lamb whom Guerchy has driven mad,
by trying to *precipitate into the river of oblivion.*"
This phrase depicts d'Eon admirably. In an ordinary
position he would have lived unperceived, above all,
since his scandalous quarrel with the Count de
Guerchy had shut him out from every official career.†

---

* An antiquary of Tonnerre, d'Eon's native place, M. Le Maistre,
who is at present preparing a serious work on the chevalier, with the
same documents which were made use of by Gaillardet, writes to
tell us that we were not wrong in mistrusting the pretended discovery
of the latter in reference to d'Eon's relations with the Queen of
England, and that all this story is a *pure romance.* As far as Beaumarchais is concerned, we could, for our part, easily point out
numerous inaccuracies in M. Gaillardet's work.

† It is known that in 1765, d'Eon, then Secretary of Legation at
London, had gone so far as to accuse his ambassador publicly, before
the English courts, of having attempted to poison and assassinate him.

Passing for a woman, or for a being apart, whose sex was a mystery, he was sure to attract general attention. This stratagem was successful, since it gained for him a celebrity which is not always attained by lofty natures and noble actions.* After his return to France, d'Eon circulated a report that Beaumarchais had retained for his own use a portion of the money destined for himself. The latter complained of it to M. de Vergennes, who replied to him in the following letter, which he authorised him to publish :—

"Versailles, January 10, 1778.

"I have received, Sir, your letter of the third of this month, and could only read with much surprise that you heard that Mademoiselle d'Eon accused you of having appropriated, to her prejudice, money which she supposed was destined for her. I can hardly think, Sir, that this young lady could have made so calumnious an accusation; but, if she made it, you must not be at all uneasy and affected by it. You have the pledge and proof of your innocence in the account you rendered of your conduct in the most approved

---

* The same motive of vanity can explain his persistence, until death, in this disguise, after he had once adopted it. A distinguished man, who knew him in London during the latter period, has furnished me with another explanation. According to him, d'Eon, after having first of all found the female costume very inconvenient, had at last, however, accustomed himself to it, and wore it by inclination; always, however, mixing with it something of the masculine dress. The same person, who kindly gave me this information, assures me that, if in 1809, people in France still believed in d'Eon's being of the feminine sex, in England none of those persons who, at this period, associated with the chevalier doubted his being a man.

form, based upon authentic documents, and in the recogni-
tion of your services which I gave you with the knowledge
of the king. Far from your disinterested conduct being open
to suspicion, I do not forget, Sir, that you have made no
claim for your personal expenses, and that I never saw you
exhibit any other design than that of facilitating Mademoiselle d'Eon's return to her country.

"I am very perfectly, Sir, your very humble and very
obedient servant,

"DE VERGENNES."

Beaumarchais, indeed, had not on this occasion
even claimed his travelling expenses; indeed he could
afford at this time to be generous towards the
government, for the government was still more so
towards him. He had at last reached his end. By
continually rendering trifling services in trifling
affairs, he had attained a sufficient hold on the confidence of Louis XVI., of M. de Maurepas, and of M.
de Vergennes, to overcome scruples and hesitations
as to their policy in the American question. Under
the influence of his ardent solicitations, the government had decided to give their secret support to the
insurgent colonies, and to intrust the important and
delicate mission to him. On the 10th June 1776,
Beaumarchais had obtained from the king a million
francs, with which he set up and commenced that
great American transaction, in which he will be seen
to display a talent for organisation and extension of
views, a power of will, which the reader will be

astonished perhaps to find in the author of "The Barber of Seville." In the meanwhile, it must also be remembered, in order to form a just opinion of the epoch, that at this same date of June 10, 1776, when Beaumarchais was receiving from the government such a proof of confidence, and was becoming the agent and depository of a state secret, the discovery of which might one day kindle war between France and England, he was still under the effect of the judgment passed upon him by the Maupeou Parliament. The person whom the government commissioned to carry succour to the Americans, and who was soon to make war on his own account against the English, was in a certain way civilly dead. These contradictory positions could not, however, continue; before fitting out his ships, the convict of the Maupeou Parliament had to set about regaining his rights of citizenship.

CHAPTER XVI.

RECALL OF THE OLD PARLIAMENT.—RESTITUTION OF
CIVIL RIGHTS.—THE ADVOCATE GENERAL.—DISSO-
LUTION OF THE PARLIAMENT.

THOROUGHLY understanding his epoch, Beaumarchais had felt that the principal thing for him to
do, was not to insist on the justice of his cause,
but, in the first instance, to make himself useful,
and then necessary, after which his rehabilitation would accomplish itself. While he was wear-
ing out post-horses in the service of the king, he
had for the first time the satisfaction of hearing
that the Maupeou Parliament, which had struck
him so cruel a blow, had died in its turn, of
the wounds it had received from him. After the
accession of Louis XVI., this judicial body had fallen
into such a state of judicial degradation, that when
some of its members complained to old Maurepas,
the head of the new ministry, of being no longer
able to go to the sitting without being insulted by
the people, the minister had replied to them, with
the levity which characterised himself and the epoch;

" Well, go then in dominoes, you will not be recognised." This answer sufficiently indicated the fate reserved for Maupeou's magistrates; their dismissal, however, was delayed six months longer. It was not until November 12, 1774, that an edict of Louis XVI. abolished the new magistracy, and recalled the old Parliament. On the 25th of the same month, Beaumarchais wrote to M. de Sartines:

"I hope you do not wish me to remain with the *blame* upon me of this villanous Parliament, which you have just buried beneath the ruins of its dishonour. The whole of Europe has well avenged me for this odious and absurd judgment; but that is not sufficient: I must have a decree destroying the sentence. I am going to work for it, but with the moderation of a man who no longer fears either intrigue or injustice. I wait your good offices towards this important end."

In spite of the intentions expressed in this letter, Beaumarchais did not hurry himself, for he waited nearly two years longer; but, when he considered the proper moment had arrived, when his credit was assured, when M. de Maurepas was completely captivated by him, he attacked the difficulty with his usual impetuosity, and carried it with a rush. It was two years since the sentence had been made final. He might have obtained its abolition by letters-royal, but did not wish to do so. It was not an act of pardon, but one of justice that he demanded; and it was necessary the restored Parliament should destroy the work of the

bastard Parliament, which had usurped its functions.
Louis XVI. granted him first of all, Letters Patent,
dated August 12, 1776, which relieved him of the
time lapsed since the signing of the judgment, 26th
February 1774. " Considering," says the royal Act,
" that our beloved friend, Pierre-Augustin Caron de
Beaumarchais, left the kingdom by our orders, and
in our service, it is our will that he be replaced and
re-established, in such and a like state as if the said
lapse of time had not passed by, and that he may,
notwithstanding the said lapse, appeal against the
said judgment, either by a civil petition, or by such
other legal channel as he may think good."

It only remained to obtain *lettres de requête civile*,
that is to say a new royal Act, referring Beaumarchais to the Parliament, for the legal annulment of
the judgment pronounced against him. Now, this
application had to be submitted to the grand council,
which, as will be remembered, had formed part of
the Maupeou Parliament, and in which, after the
destruction of the Parliament, the greater number of
Beaumarchais' judges had re-entered. Beaumarchais,
obliged to quit Paris for Bordeaux, where he was to
organise his American scheme, did not wish to go
until the application had been admitted. " Go all the
same," said the minister Maurepas. " The council can
give its decision without you." He started for Bordeaux with Gudin. The second day after his arrival

he learned that his petition had been rejected by the grand council.

"'Sixty hours afterwards,' relates Gudin, in his manuscript, 'we were at Paris.' 'What!' said Beaumarchais, to the Count de Maurepas, who was rather surprised to see him again so soon, 'whilst I hasten to the extremities of France for the affairs of the king, you ruin mine at Versailles.' 'It is a stupidity of Miromesnil's,'* replied M. de Maurepas. 'Go and find him; tell him I wish to speak to him, and return together.' They had an explanation, all three together; the affair was taken up in another form, for there were forms for all cases, foreseen and unforeseen. The council formed an entirely different opinion, and the application was granted."

Here a new subject of embarrassment arose: it was the end of the month of August; the vacation of the Parliaments was commencing, and that body would not legislate on the application until the vacation was over; but Beaumarchais did not adjourn so easily an affair which he had once commenced. He went to find M. de Maurepas again, and being convinced that a man's interests are never so well taken care of as by himself, he did with the first minister what we have seen him do with the king. He prepared a note for the Chief President and for the Attorney-General, had the note copied, and signed in duplicate by M. de Maurepas, and sent it off; it is conceived in the following terms:

---

* The Minister of Justice.

"Versailles, 27th August, 1776.

"The department of the king's affairs, with which M. de Beaumarchais is entrusted, obliges him to start on a journey without delay. He is afraid of leaving Paris before his petition is granted. He assures me that it may be attended to before the vacation. I ask for no favour as regards the decision itself, but merely to lose no time in arriving at it. You will thus oblige him,

"Who has the honour to be, &c.,

"MAUREPAS."

This was still not sufficient for Beaumarchais; he wished the Advocate-General Séguier to speak and use his eloquence on his behalf; hence another letter to M. de Maurepas, accompanied by a fresh note, written in rather clearer terms, to M. Séguier, which note the minister copied with the same docility as the preceding one. Here is, first of all, the insinuating letter addressed to the old minister :—

"Paris, August 30, 1776.

"M. le Comte,—I should go to you and throw myself at your feet this morning, if I had not a settled *rendez-vous* at the Spanish Ambassador's.* It is very gratifying to my heart to see that the respect which is offered you renders every one proud and jealous of doing something to please you. M. Séguier, learning that you had had the kindness to recommend the Chief President and the Attorney-General to use despatch in my affair, could not avoid saying, to one of his

* For the American affair. The Spanish Government had joined the French Government, and was also preparing to give its secret support to the Americans.

friends, who is also one of mine, 'Such a recommendation would have made me very eloquent in this affair.' Oh, human nature! Never grow tired, M. le Comte of doing good actions. . . . I only request your signature to the accompanying letter, and your seal on the envelope: instantly my affair acquires wings, and I shall have to thank you for having hastened by three months the recovery of my citizenship, which I ought never to have lost.

"I am, with the most respectful gratitude, &c.,

"BEAUMARCHAIS."

Now comes the letter to the Advocate-General Séguier, written by Beaumarchais, and signed by M. de Maurepas:

"Versailles, 30th August, 1776.

"I learnt, Sir, from M. de Beaumarchais, that if you do not have the kindness to speak in his affair, it is impossible for him to obtain a judgment between now and September 7. The department of the king's affairs, with which M. de Beaumarchais is entrusted, requires|him to start on a journey without delay; he is afraid of leaving Paris before being restored to his citizenship, and he has so long suffered from being deprived of it, that his desire is legitimate enough. I ask for no favour as regards the decision itself, but you will oblige me exceedingly if you contribute to getting it decided before the holidays.

"I have the honour to be,

"Very truly, &c.,

"MAUREPAS." *

---

* It is seen that the recommendation becomes here more direct, in spite of the conventional restriction which accompanies it

It is here seen how much Beaumarchais' situation has changed since the Goëzman law-suit. He has not only public opinion on his side, he has also the governing powers, which, however, does not prevent his cultivating the favour of the multitude with the same care as before; for whilst he takes his precautions with regard to the ministry, and secures the official support of the Advocate-General, he at the same time chooses to defend him, a barrister, who had stood almost alone in constantly refusing to plead before the Maupeou Parliaments, and whom this constant opposition had rendered very popular, the Advocate Target. In entrusting his defence to him, Beaumarchais, always faithful to his theatrical tastes, wrote a letter to him, which circulated everywhere, and which commenced in these words :—

"The martyr, Beaumarchais, to the Virgin Target." The Virgin Target, who with his somewhat empty but pompous and sonorous eloquence, undertook to maintain the popularity of Goëzman's ancient adversary, and to defend him by associating his cause with that of the restoration of the Parliament and liberty regained :—

"Fulfil then at length, gentlemen," said Target, in concluding his speech, "fulfil the general expectation, and, I venture to say, the wishes you have yourselves secretly formed for the reparation of injustice. Absolved by the public, it is time M. de Beaumarchais be delivered by the law. The period has passed of contradictions and disturbances, in which the citizen did not always look into the decisions of his judges for the guidance of his own judgments. Union is re-established, the nation at last possesses its magistrates. The ministers, the depositaries of the laws, have regained their right, greater and more honourable than ever, of being the arbiters of morals and the moderators of sentiments. In the bosom of this happy concord, beneath the eye of the public, and the hands of the law, M. de Beaumarchais is about to resume, as a right which belongs to him, this first wealth of man living in a state of society, the honour which in awaiting the return of order he had left as a trust to public opinion."

After Target's address, the Advocate-General also spoke in favour of the rehabilitation; and, on the 6th of September, 1776, a solemn decree of the entire Parliament, Grand Chamber and Tournelle assembled, annulled the judgment passed against Beaumarchais by the Maupeou Parliament, restored him to his civil rights and the functions he had previously occupied. This decree was received with the most lively enthusiasm by the mob, who encumbered the court, and the happy suitor was borne in triumph, in the midst of applause, from the grand chamber to his carriage. He had prepared a discourse, which he intended to pronounce before that of Target's; he was prevailed upon to renounce his intention; but, as he was anxious to set himself right with public opinion, he published it the following day. This speech, which appears in his works, is a good specimen of the dignified style, but is above all very clever and very

bold. It has been seen with what ingenuity Beaumarchais could take advantage of a minister's favour;
but, while using his credit with M. de Maurepas, he
did not give up his character of citizen and defender
of the rights of the nation. In his discourse to the
Parliament, he not only yielded nothing to his former
adversaries, who for the most part were still members
of the grand council, but he maintained all his attacks against the forms and rules of their administration of justice. Now these forms and these rules, as
M. Saint Marc-Girardin justly remarks, "did not
belong in particular to the Maupeou Parliament;
they belonged also to the old Parliament." The blows
which Beaumarchais had given to the first, were destined to rebound to the second. In attacking secresy
in the administration of justice, in attacking all the
modes of questioning, of examination, of re-examina-
tion which prolonged and confused the actions, the repeated references, the audiences which put the suitor
at the discretion of the reporter, the secretaries
whom each suitor had to pay largely, the decisions
without foundation by which a tribunal determined
with closed doors as to the honour, the fortune, or the
life of a citizen, without other explanation than this
formula: "For the circumstances proved by the trial."
Beaumarchais by combating these various abuses, and
convincing the masses of the necessity of a judicial
reform; Beaumarchais, after helping to destroy the

Maupeou Parliament amid the applause of the old Parliament, contributed, without being aware of it himself, to prepare at the same time the ruin of the Parliament which had applauded him. When indeed these proud legislators, seated up in their places, were seen to continue their former errors, when, after a systematic opposition which was conducted with equal ardour against good and against evil, they were seen to demand the convocation of the states-general, but to endeavour to annul their action beforehand by limiting it within old forms, so as to secure for themselves a sort of dictatorship, the same unpopularity which had thrown out the Maupeou magistrates, turned them out in their turn. After having made kings recoil, they were summoned to the bar of the constituent assembly, and it was there signified to them, in the words of Beaumarchais, "that the nation was the judge of the judges." Some days afterwards, a simple decree decided that the Parliament had ceased to exist, and the Mayor Bailly came to place the seals on the doors of those judgment halls from which the signal had arisen of the crisis which was agitating France. Thus, in his struggle against Goëzman, Beaumarchais had been an involuntary, but powerful instrument of the revolution; he was the same, when happy and proud of the victory which at last gave him back his citizen's rights, he threw himself body and soul into his great American enter-

prise.   Before following him in it, it should not be
forgotten that he always directed several enterprises
at the same time, and at the moment when he was
preparing his forty vessels, he was getting " The Barber
of Seville " performed.

CHAPTER XVII.

WITH "The Barber of Seville," Beaumarchais entered, as dramatic author, upon the path of great successes, and at the same time of great tribulations. His first comedy, before it could be produced on the stage, met with almost as many obstacles as the second, and underwent divers transformations, of which some account must be given.

Played for the first time in February 1775, " The Barber" had been composed in 1772; it was at first a comic opera, in the style of the period, which the author destined for the *Italian* comedians, as they were called, who then possessed the privilege of playing works of this kind.* The complete failure

* What was then called the Comédie Italienne, did not resemble either our Italian Theatre or our Opéra-Comique. It was a Theatre of a mixed kind, between the Comédie-Française and the Theatre de

of his second drama, "The Two Friends," and the taste he always had for couplets, drove Beaumarchais from one·extreme to the other, from the sentimental style to comic pieces with songs. The originality of "The Barber of Seville" in its first form, consisted principally in the fact, that the author of the words was at the same time the composer, or at least the arranger of the music. It will be remembered that in his letters from Madrid, while expressing a marked disdain for the Spanish Theatre in general, Beaumarchais entertained a very lively enthusiasm for the Spanish music, and above all, for the interludes sung under the name of *tonadillas* or *saynètes*. The recollection of the *tonadillas* appears to have given risê to "The Barber of Seville." It was first written, in order to introduce some Spanish airs, which the author had brought from Madrid, and was arranging in the French style. "I compose," he writes at this epoch, "airs to my words, and words to my airs." Whether Beaumar-

Nicolet.[7] Sometimes farces, taken from the Italian *répertoire*, were played there; sometimes comic operas, of a much simpler nature than those of our own, and which in general were *vaudevilles*, with couplets rather than musical compositions of an elaborate nature. Here, for the rest, is a bill which I extract from the "Journal de Paris," of 1779, which will prove that even at this epoch the Comédie Italienne was still alternating between farces in the Italian style and comic operas :—" The Italian comedians," says this bill, "will give to-day ' Les Défis d'Arlequin et de Scapin,' an Italian comedy; to-morrow ' Les Evénements imprévus,' and ' Rose et Colas.' "

chais' Spanish airs did not seduce the ears of the actors of the Comédie Italienne, or whether they considered the work had too much resemblance to Sedaine's opera, "On ne s'avise jamais de tout," which was played on the same stage in 1761, it is quite certain that "The Barber of Seville," as a comic opera, was refused point blank by the Italian actors in 1772.* Gudin, in his unpublished Memoirs, attributes this refusal to the principal actor, Clairval, who had commenced life as a barber, and who, after representing Figaro in the shops of Paris, had an invincible antipathy for every part which reminded him of his original profession. Beaumarchais was obliged then, to give up all idea of having his comic opera performed. I could only find some shreds of it among his papers, which lead me to think that it

---

* The manuscript of the comedy of "The Barber," contains several allusions to this refusal, which were suppressed at the second representation. Thus, in one passage, Figaro said—"I have written a comic opera which had only a 'quarter of a failure,' at Madrid." "What do you mean by a 'quarter of a failure?'" asked Almaviva. "Sir," replied Figaro, "I mean that I only failed before the comic senate of the stage; they spared me an entire failure by refusing to act my piece." He then gave one of the airs of the comic opera of the same name:—

> "J'aime mieux être un bon barbier,
> Traînant ma poudreuse mantille.
> Tout bon auteur de son métier
> Est souvent forcé de piller,
> Grapiller,
> Houspiller," &c.

was no great loss, as the author's poetic talent was
very unequal, and rarely produced two good couplets
in succession, while his musical talent did not rise
above that of an amateur. It was reserved for two
great masters, Mozart and Rossini, to add the charm
of music to the inspirations of Beaumarchais. As for
himself, after being rejected as a librettist and arranger of Spanish music, he determined to transform
his opera into a comedy for the Théâtre Français.

Accepted by this theatre, after receiving the ap-
probation of the censor Marin, "The Barber of
Séville" was going to be played in February 1773,
when the quarrel of the author with the Duke de
Chaulnes, which we have already narrated, took place.
Beaumarchais was sent to For-l'Evêque, where he
remained two months and a half, and the representation of his piece was necessarily adjourned. He was
preparing to produce it a second time after leaving
his prison, when the criminal accusation was insti-
tuted by Councillor Goëzman against him, and
"The Barber of Seville" was adjourned again. Meanwhile the immense success of the Memorials against
Goëzman having made the suitor very popular, the
French comedians wished to profit by that circumstance. They solicited permission to play "The Barber," and obtained it; the representation was
announced for the 12th February 1774. "All the
boxes," says Grimm, "were let, up to the fifth

representation." Just then, on Thursday, February the 10th, an order from high authority appeared, to cover over the bills, and stop the representation. That same day, February the 10th, Beaumarchais published the last and most brilliant of his judicial *factums*. As the report had been spread that his piece was full of allusions to his law-suit, he added to the end of his last Memorial a note, in which, after announcing to the public that "The Barber of Seville" had been prohibited, he disclaimed all the allusions attributed to him, and terminated thus:

"I beg the court to be kind enough to order the manuscript of my piece, as it was deposited with the police more than a year since, and as it was going to be played, to be laid before it; subjecting myself to all the rigour of the law, if in the composition or style of the work, anything be found having the smallest reference to the unhappy law-suit which M. Goëzman has brought against me, or which is contrary to the profound respect I profess for the Parliament.

"CARON DE BEAUMARCHAIS."

The fact is, that at this epoch, the comedy of "The Barber," which had been composed before the Goëzman law-suit, contained no allusion whatever to it. Although in its original form, it was simply characterised by gaiety, and had nothing of an absolutely satirical nature, it bore the punishment of the reputation which was given to it before-hand, and Beaumarchais could not obtain permission to have it played. Soon afterwards, the different

missions of which we have spoken, took him to
England and Germany, and he had to throw his
comedy on one side for a time. However, he did
not forget it; the very obstacles which were opposed
to him, rendered him, as was always the case, more
obstinate in surmounting them. On his return from
Vienna, in December 1774, at the end of his month's
captivity, which gave him some right to a sort of
compensation, he was more urgent than ever in re-
questing permission to represent his piece. Circumstances were favourable: the Maupeou Parliament
had ceased to exist for a month, Louis XV. was no
more, the manuscript which Beaumarchais presented was very inoffensive; he at length obtained
permission to have "The Barber" represented. But,
between the permission and the representation, he
acted as he thought fit: this comedy had been prohibited on account of pretended allusions, which did
not exist; he made up for this unjust prohibition by
inserting in it precisely all the allusions which the
authorities had been afraid of, and which were not
in it. He strengthened it with a great number of
satirical reflections, and a multitude of allusions
more or less audacious. He also added much to its
length, increased it by an act, in fine, overlaid it so
completely, that it fell flat before the public, the day
of its first representation. Before being able to compare the manuscript of "The Barber" in five acts,

which I have before me, and which was used on the
the first representation, I thought, as is generally
thought from the printed preface of "The Barber,"
that this piece had been originally composed in five
acts. This is an error; the original text was in four
acts, like the final text, from which it otherwise
differs very much in several respects. The manuscript of "The Barber," deposited in the archives of
the Comédie Français, is precisely this primitive text,
not yet modified by Beaumarchais for the first representation. It neither corresponds with the piece as it
was played for the first time, nor with the piece as
it is printed; * but like the printed piece it is in
four acts, and the priority of the manuscript in question is established by the following note, written by
Beaumarchais' hand on the last leaf.

"I declare that the present manuscript is perfectly similar
to the one which has been submitted to the censorship of M.
Artaud, after having been submitted, more than a year ago,
to that of M. Marin, and perfectly similar to the one which
is in the hands of M. de Sartines, on the examination of
which the French comedians have twice, without avail, received permission to represent the piece. I accordingly beg
Monseigneur the Prince de Conti to be kind enough to keep

* I am indebted for the manuscript of the "Théâtre-Française,"
which it was important for me to compare with my own, to the
kindness of one of the associates of this theatre, M. Régnier, who is
not only an artist of eminent talent, but who is also a man of learning
and taste, well versed in the history of dramatic literature, and taking
an amiable and sympathetic interest in all conscientious labours.

it, so as to oppose it to all other manuscript or printed version of the piece, which might be circulated with additions, made to injure me, of things that have never been either in my head or my piece. Protesting that I disavow every version that is not exactly similar to the present manuscript.

"CARON DE BEAUMARCHAIS.

"Paris, March 10, 1774."

On the first page of the same manuscript in four acts, the following words, written by Beaumarchais, can also be read :—

"Manuscript of the author, from which alone the piece will be played, if it is ever played at all.

"CARON DE BEAUMARCHAIS."

This declaration, in March 1774, was sincere, but it was made in accordance with the necessity of the case ; in February 1775, the circumstances were no longer the same, Beaumarchais paid no more attention to his declaration than if he had never made it, and effected considerable alterations in his piece. None of these alterations are found in the manuscript containing the two notes which we have just quoted. But although this manuscript, which according to one of the two notes must have belonged to the Prince de Conti, is the only text of "The Barber" preserved in the archives of the Théâtre Français, it is evident that this is not the text which was used at the first representation of the piece, as it is in four acts, and every one knows that "The Barber" was represented for the first time in five. Nor is this manuscript the text as finally re-arranged in four acts, and as it was printed, for it differs considerably from the printed text. It is simply, then, the text of this comedy, as arranged at first in four acts. A second manuscript, which I found among Beaumarchais' papers, gives "The Barber of Seville," after being remodelled by the author in 1775, divided into five acts, and in the state in which it was played for the first time.

By comparing the two texts of "The Barber," we can follow, with some exactness, the somewhat curious working of Beaumarchais' mind beneath the influence of the changes produced in his situation by the Goëzman law-suit, and also beneath the influence of the failure of his piece at the first representation. In the original manuscript in four acts of the Comédie Française, the composition of which dates from the end of 1772, and which consequently preceded the Goëzman law-suit, the piece is purely and simply an imbroglio, in the lively style, of worse contruction than that of the printed text, containing many lengthy passages, and presenting more traces of the old *opera comique;* for instance, it has three additional songs, which contain a sufficiently large number of allusions in bad taste, and tinged generally with a coarse humour, which gives it more resemblance to farce. On the other hand, the allusions and satirical reflections are much rarer than in the published text, and the piece does not yet present that philosophic and incisive character which begins to manifest itself in "The Barber" as it was printed, and which was afterwards much more marked in "The Marriage of Figaro."

The manuscript modified, and augmented by one act for the first representation, is much more overlaid in every way, than the two texts of which we have just spoken; Beaumarchais had not restrained himself. The man who had become celebrated by means of a law-suit which had gained for him great *éclât*, was going over a piece which had been composed at an epoch when he was still but little known, and when he had not had to defend himself against inveterate enemies. The recent agitations of his life can be traced in the alterations made in his comedy. Thus, for example, the famous tirade on "la calomnie," which Beaumarchais put in the mouth of Basil, and which is one of the most brilliant and significant bits of "The Barber," is not found in the original manuscript of the Théâtre Français; it was added afterwards, in 1775, to the manuscript which was used at the first representation, by means of a leaf pasted upon it, written entirely and without a single interruption in the hand of Beaumarchais. The comic author felt compelled to avenge the suitor. In the original manuscript, Basil, reproaching Bartholo with not having given him enough money, contented himself with saying to him, in musical language,

"You have been mean about the expenses, and in the harmony of good order, an *unequal marriage*, an evident illegality, are dissonances, which ought always to be prepared and prevented by the common chord of gold." In the manuscript, as altered for the first representation, Beaumarchais, between the words *an unequal marriage—an evident illegality*, has added, with his own hand, the words: *an iniquitous decision*, which have become part of the printed text. Here again is the man, condemned by the Maupeou Parliament protesting and avenging himself. Almaviva's speech to Figaro, "Do you know that a person has only twenty-four hours at the Palais for cursing *his judges*," and Figaro's answer, "He has twenty-four years on the stage," are also not found in the manuscript of the Comédie Français. Figaro's biography, related by himself at the commencement of the piece, has also undergone minor alterations, such, among others, as the following. In the manuscript of the Théâtre Français, Figaro said: "Welcomed in one town, imprisoned in another, and everywhere superior to events." . . . In the manuscript of 1775, the man who had been condemned to "blame," by the Maupeou Parliament, has added with his hand: "Praised on one side, blamed on the other." In the same tirade, Figaro in enumerating the enemies of men of letters, said: "The insects, the mosquitoes, the critics, the censors, and everything that attaches

itself to the skin of unfortunate men of letters." In
the altered manuscript of 1775, he adds a new insect,
les maringouins. This burlesque denomination, which
is also preserved in the printed text, is evidently a
passing stroke for Marin.

In the same manuscript, as altered in 1775, it can
be seen that Beaumarchais was very desirous to
change the appellation of that type of meanness, cu-
pidity, and cunning, which, before his law-suit, he
had entitled Basil: he has in many places marked
out the name, and replaced it by that of Guzman, in
allusion to Goëzman; then finally, not venturing to
go so far, he has given up the notion and re-written
Basil. At a later period, we shall see him again take
the name of Guzman which pleases him, and make
the allusion clearer by applying it not to a musician,
but to a vile, avaricious, and foolish judge, whom he
will name Don Guzman Brid'oison.

Sometimes the alterations of 1775 relate to the
character of Figaro, to which the author adds features
from his own physiognomy, as in the following passage, which was interpolated at the first representation, but afterwards suppressed, and which figures
neither in the manuscript of the Théâtre Français,
nor in the printed text. Bartholo, in his dispute
with Figaro, said to him: " Vous vous mêlez de trop
de choses, Monsieur." Figaro answered: " Que vous
en chaut si je m'en démêle, Monsieur?" "And all this

might have a bad end, Sir," resumed Bartholo. "Yes for all those who threaten others, Sir," answered Figaro. This Figaro, who meddles with too many things (*se mêle de trop de choses*), but who gets out of them always (*s'en démêle toujours*), was too manifestly related to Beaumarchais, and that was probably what determined him to suppress this detail.

In the original manuscript of the Théâtre Français, when Bartholo was quarrelling with his servants, one of them, La Jeunesse, said to him "Ah, but what reason is there, Sir?" Bartholo cried out, "It is very fine for you wretches to talk about reason; I am your master, *pour avoir toujours raison.*" In the altered text, Beaumarchais has replaced the word "reason" in the two first instances, by the word "justice," which makes Bartholo say, "It is very fine for you wretches to talk about justice," and he completes his thought with the following still more daring passage, which has remained in the printed piece, and which is not in the manuscript of the Théâtre Français. La Jeunesse replies to Bartholo, "But *pardi*, when a thing is true!" Bartholo answers, "When a thing is true! If I do not wish it to be true, I maintain that it is not true. Only allow all these scoundrels to be in the right, you will soon see what will become of authority." We shall further on see that Beaumarchais wished particularly to retain this passage.

In the original text of "The Barber," in the last

scene, the author only introduced a notary; in the altered manuscript of 1775, Beaumarchais added to the notary a judge, and not daring to call him by his name, calls him at first, "*un homme de loi*," he then marked out the words "*homme de loi*," and used the Spanish word "alcalde," which gave the same idea without being attended with the same inconveniences. Finally, in the *dénouemont*, he introduced a dialogue between Figaro and the alcalde, in which the former rallied the latter with astonishing effrontery. This scene was considered too strong, and contributed to the failure of "The Barber" on its first representation. Beaumarchais suppressed it at the second, and it does not figure in the printed text; but as Beaumarchais did not like to lose what he considered good, he reproduced this passage nine years later, somewhat softened, in "The Marriage of Figaro." It is the one in which Figaro, recognised by Brid'oison, asks insolently after his wife and son, "the youngest who," he says, "is a very pretty child, I flatter myself." The scene was at first in "The Barber of Sevllle;" it was, indeed, even stronger, and rendered with a greater crudity of expression, but fundamentally it was the same scene. After being hissed in 1775, it went on very well in 1784.

The same observation applies to the well known tirade of "The Marriage of Figaro," on "*goddam*, the basis of the English language." This tirade was

originally in "The Barber of Seville;" Beaumarchais
had added it to his second manuscript in the scene
where Figaro and Almaviva recognise one another;
it was also rejected by the public in 1775, as too
forced, and too much like burlesque. Beaumarchais
withdrew it, but made it over intrepidly to "The
Marriage of Figaro," where it had much success,
and where it still enjoys the privilege of amusing the
pit. Under the influence of "The Barber of Seville"
itself, and from other more general causes, the public
taste had become modified between 1775 and 1784; it
had become less and less particular about the distinction of classes and styles.* In order to complete

* The tirade on *goddam*, in "The Barber of Seville," was connected with the rest of the scene in the following manner :—Figaro
was relating that he had travelled in England, after which he delivered
this tirade. Almaviva replied to him—"With so much knowledge
you might traverse the whole of Europe." *Figaro.*—"Accordingly,
to come back, I have traversed France with much pleasure, for I also
know the principal woods of that country." Here the ground became dangerous. Beaumarchais, after pointing out the difficulty,
evaded it, by means of these words of Almaviva—"Spare me your
erudition, and finish your story." *Figaro.*—"On my return to Madrid
I wished to make another essay of my literary talents; I composed
two dramas." *Almaviva.*—"Mercy!" *Figaro.*—"Is it the style or the
author that your excellency disdains?" *Almaviva.*—"I hear too much
said against the style, for it not to have something to be said in its
favour." This quotation will be sufficient for those who remember
the printed text of "The Barber," to perceive that in the text of the
first representation, Beaumarchais put himself in the piece in a much
more direct manner, and ventured nearer with his allusions. In
another passage, when the Count called Figaro back, Beaumarchais

this comparison between the three texts of "The Barber of Seville,". after speaking of the passages which Beaumarchais strengthened in the original manuscript, and those which he held over, we must say a word as to those which he was obliged to cut out altogether after the first representation. The opportunity of studying a celebrated author through an intimate knowledge of his mode of composition, his erasures, his substitutions, and his rough drafts, is rarely presented; and it is, perhaps, the most certain means of arriving at a just idea of the qualities, good and bad, of his intellect.

With his determination to restore the old Gallic humour, Beaumarchais did not fear to push comedy to the limits of farce; but as he also wished to please refined intellects, and as, moreover, an author can never completely escape the influence of his epoch, the result was, that this declared enemy of all that was strained and affected in ideas and language, was often pretentious and modish. These two faults of a contrary nature, pretentiousness and triviality, of which traces are still found in the charming comedy of "The Barber" as we possess it, were much more marked in the text of the first representation. To quote one

made the latter answer—*Ques-a-co?* (what is that?) This reminiscence of his adversary Marin, was looked upon, in 1775, as too direct a personality. Beaumarchais withdrew the *ques-a-co*, but again replaced it in "The Marriage of Figaro."

example alone, at the opening of the piece, Almaviva, walking about under Rosina's windows, said at first, as in the printed piece: "Follow a woman at Seville, when Madrid and the court offer such easy pleasures! Eh! that is just what I am avoiding;" he then added this metaphorical, elaborated, and unequal sentence: "All our valleys are full of myrtle, every one can gather some of it with ease; one plant alone grows in the distance on the slope of the rock, it pleases me, not that it is more beautiful, but fewer persons can reach it." This "myrtle" and this "rock" having doubtless had no success at the first representation Beaumarchais gave them up, and Almaviva's monologue became by the suppression, much more natural and flowing. By the side of these affected passages, the manuscript of the first representation of "The Barber" contains many others, in which the author seems to have made it his object to carry coarse pleasantry as far as possible. For instance, in the scene where Almaviva and Figaro recognise one another, Beaumarchais began by enriching the original text with a new stroke, which has been preserved in the printed text. "I did not recognise you," says Almaviva to Figaro, "you are so stout and fat!" "What can you expect, Monseigneur?" replies Figaro, "it is poverty." Hitherto the sally was good, but the author spoiled it directly afterwards by forcing it, for Figaro added these words

"Not to mention that I have lost all my fathers and mothers; since last year I have become a complete orphan by the death of the last." Thus to an amusing pleasantry succeeded a gross piece of burlesque, which was justly suppressed after the first representation.* Further on Figaro said: "I passed the night gaily, *avec trois ou quatre buveurs de mes voisines.*"

The project of reviving, at the same time as the old comedy, the old language, that of Rabelais, and also, to some extent, that of the booths, is also very clearly indicated in the manuscript of the first representation. It is known that in the printed text of "The Barber," Figaro, giving to Almaviva the portrait of the old guardian who wishes to marry Rosina, represents him thus: "C'est un beau, gros, court, jeune vieillard, gris-pommelé, rusé, rasé, blasé, qui guette, et furète, et gronde, et geint tout à la fois." This portrait with its repetition of epithets, in which

---

* It is rather a singular thing that Beaumarchais, whose excellent qualities are now known, both as a son and a brother, and who afterwards shows himself to be the best of fathers, should have allowed himself to be led away by a systematic intention of creating the type of a universal jester, so far as to make Figaro apply his raillery to a class of sentiments which even comedy usually respects. Figaro is not malevolent, but it is part of the author's plan that he shall take a serious view of nothing, neither paternity nor even maternity. Hence those scenes, which are truly shocking, of the "Folle Journée," between Figaro, Marceline, and Bartholo. If it can be said that Figaro offers points of resemblance to Beaumarchais, it is certainly not on that side.

the imitation of Rabelais is already perceptible, is only a fragment of the more detailed portrait of Bartholo, which the piece contained at the first representation, and which was in the following terms: "C'est un beau, gros, court, jeune vieillard, gris-pommelé, rasé, rusé, blasé, frisqué et guerdonné comme amoureux en baptême, à la vérité; mais ridé, chassieux, jaloux, sottin, goutteux, marmiteux, qui tousse, et crache, et gronde, et geint tour à tour. Gravelle aux reins, perclus d'un bras et déferré des jambes; le pauvre écuyer! S'il verdoie encore par le chef, vous sentez que c'est comme la mousse ou le gui sur un arbre mort; quel attisement pour un tel feu!"

This portrait of Rosina was in the same Rabelaisian tone, which was now scarcely found anywhere except in the booths of the boulevards. There were also scenes in which the license of language was extreme, especially one in which Basil, when consulted by Bartholo as to his marriage with Rosina, recited to him with the most daring variations, Pibrac's famous quatrain upon old men who marry young wives. All these additions having lengthened the original manuscript considerably, which was already too long, Beaumarchais had been led to add another act to it, by dividing the third into two; but the division was of the most unfortunate kind, and, it can be easily understood, contributed to the failure which the comedy at first experienced. The fourth act commenced in the middle of the third, when Rosina has just sung the little arietta which is now omitted.

Quand dans la plaine
L'amour ramène
Le printemps, etc.

Almaviva disguised as the music-master, and waiting for Figaro, after saying to Rosina, as in the printed piece, "Let us while away the time," continued the dialogue in this manner:

"And the fine obligato recitative which follows the piece, do you sing that also, Madame?

"ROSINA.—Yes; but it must be accompanied by the harpsichord, on account of the frequent *ritornelli*.

"BARTHOLO.—Ah! let us go to the harpsichord, for there is nothing in the world so important as the *ritornelli*."

Now the harpsichord, by a somewhat poor device, instead of being in the room in which they had just sung, was in an adjacent closet. The two lovers, after trying in vain to induce Bartholo to listen to them from the drawing-room went with him into the closet; the curtain fell on this feeble incident, and thus ended the third act. In the fourth act Bartholo, Rosina, and the Count came in, as they had gone out. "I have not lost a syllable of it" (of the recitative) said Bartholo; "it is very fine, but she is right. That closet is positively stifling; to-morrow, I shall have my harpsichord placed in the drawing-room." And the conversation was resumed until the arrival of Figaro. This fourth act, which was made up of half the third, being found too short, Beaumarchais had interlarded it with allusions, which were given to Figaro, who, not satisfied with singing the unpublished air quoted above, made Almaviva sing other couplets, which are not worth the trouble of mentioning, and gave himself up to a multitude of pleasantries of doubtful taste, on the subject of doctors, women, and mythology.

In this unfortunate supplementary act, Beaumarchais had discovered the secret of spoiling the best scene of the whole piece, the one in which Basil sees in Bartholo, an involuntary accomplice of the deceit which had been practised upon him, uniting with Almaviva, Rosina, and Figaro, to force him to silence, and cries out " Qui diable est-ce donc qu'on trompe ici? tout le monde est dans le secret." The effect of this scene, so novel, so well led-up to, so well dialogued, was compromised by a useless extension, in which the author continued, and overdid the situation after Basil's departure.

It was in this form overlaid, exaggerated, and confused, that " The Barber of Seville " was presented for the first time to the public, February 23, 1775. The noise made by the Memorials against Goëzman was still at its height. The obstacles which had stopped the production of his comedy for two years, had redoubled the public curiosity. Beaumarchais already possessed the secret of attracting the multitude with incredible force; and, at the first representation there was an influx of spectators, which was only to be surpassed by that produced by "The Marriage of Figaro." "Never," says Grimm, speaking of "The Barber," "never did a first representation attract more people." "It was impossible" says La Harpe in his turn, in the "Correspondence," it "was impossible to appear at a moment more marked by the popular favour, or to attract a greater concourse of persons."

The effect produced on this numerous audience, was that of a very decided disappointment. People had expected a masterpiece, "it is always very difficult," writes La Harpe, at this time, "to answer to a great expectation. The piece appeared rather farcical. The length of the speeches was found wearisome, the bad jokes disgusting, the bad morals disgusting."* La Harpe's first impression, when compared with the one produced by reading the manuscript of "The Barber" as it was first represented, seems correct enough."† Beaumarchais had

* La Harpe, "Correspondance Littéraire," vol. i., p. 99.

† Grimm, who, as we have seen, was severe to contemptuousness towards Beaumarchais' dramas, apparently seduced by the talent and success of the Memorials against Goëzman, appears more indulgent than La Harpe towards "The Barber," not as it exists at present, but as it stood before being weeded and re-modelled by the author.

counted too much on his popularity; he had made too free a use in every way of his *verve,* and encumbered his piece with useless scenes and jokes, which were frequently coarse, and destroyed all its charms,

At the period when the piece was interdicted for the first time, in February 1774, Grimm, regretting the interdiction, informs his readers that he has read the manuscript. "The piece," he says, "is not only full of gaiety and *verve,* but the part of the young girl is charming in candour and interest. There are shades of delicacy and ingenuousness in the part of the Count and that of Rosina, which are really precious, and which our pit is far from being able to feel and appreciate." If this opinion is Grimm's (for in the "Correspondance," published under his name, it is not quite certain that he is always the writer); if this opinion is his, it is somewhat strange—not that candour is not to be found in the character of Rosina, but there are at the same time other shades equally marked, and not exactly shades of *delicacy and ingenuousness,* which might prevent "The Barber of Seville" being appreciated. In truth, Grimm spoke thus from seeing the original manuscript in four acts, which is better than the text in five acts; but both the first and second differ in a remarkable manner from the printed piece, and are much inferior to it. After the failure of the first representation, Grimm, who was still favourably inclined towards Beaumarchais, first of all attacked the audience. "So numerous and excited an assemblage," he writes, "always runs the risk of being tumultuous; and as the merit of the piece consists, above all, in the delicacy of the links which connect the intrigue, it required to be appreciated by a more tranquil audience." He then attacks the acting of the performers, "which had not," he said, "the ensemble and rapidity required by a comedy of this kind." Finally, he very justly gives Beaumarchais his share for having been foolish enough to make five acts out of a subject which could only furnish three or four. And, after having mentioned the suppression of one act, the excision of useless scenes, and of expressions which were out of place or in bad taste, he chronicles the success of the piece thus re-modelled.

giving to it sometimes all the character of a burlesque. The failure was complete. The author has
taken a pleasure in mentioning this failure himself
in the Preface to "The Barber," with the ease of a
man who has just performed a *tour de force*, and
who, at a day's notice, has transformed a failure
into a triumph. "You should have seen," he says,
"'The Barber's' feeble supporters disperse, hide their
faces, and take to flight. The women, always so
brave when they have anything to protect, smothered
in their *coqueluchons* up to their plumes, and lowering their eye in confusion; the men hastening to pay
visits to one another, and to make honourable
amends for what they had said in favour of my piece.
. . . . Some of them looked through their eye-
glasses to the left, as I passed by on the right, and
pretended no longer to see me. Oh! Heavens!
Others, with more courage, but making sure that
no one was looking at them, drew me into a
corner, and said to me, 'How have you produced
this illusion on our parts, for you must allow, my
friend, that your piece is the greatest platitude in
the world.'"

In writing this witty preface to "The Barber" in
its third form, which he bravely entitles "A Comedy
which was represented and failed," Beaumarchais
amuses himself at the expense of the critics, and a
little also, at the expense of the public. Like many

others of the spoiled children of celebrity, he wishes to
prove he is right precisely where he has been wrong.
Instead of confessing the transformation which was
the real cause of the ultimate success of this comedy,
he affirms with astounding *aplomb*, that scarcely anything has been changed, and that "'The Barber'
which was buried on Friday, is the same which rose
triumphantly on the Sunday." The most he ac-
knowledges is, "not being able to keep up in five
acts, he has reduced himself to four, in order to
bring back the public." The truth is, all that is
pleasing in "The Barber" as it exists now, was
certainly to be found in the piece at the first representation; but in combination with a number of faults
and careless expressions, which quite explained the
severity of the spectators. Beaumarchais exhibited
amour-propre, without reason: he wished to make
what had only been an act of justice, pass for the
effect of a cabal or a caprice on the part of the pit,
and did not think of bringing out his real merit, a
merit of a rare description, and of which I think
there are but few examples in dramatic literature.
It is not common, in effect, to see a dramatic author
take up a piece, which has been justly condemned,
and in twenty-four hours, from one day to another,
make it undergo a real metamorphosis, condense two
acts into one, transpose scenes, remove everything
that is awkward or confused in the situations and in-

trigue, suppress all that is useless, correct and enliven all that is coarse or heavy in the dialogue, and thus transform, almost instantaneously, a mediocre work into a charming production, full of movement and *verve*, in which the interest goes on constantly increasing, and of which La Harpe says, with reason, in his "Course of Literature," that it is the "best conceived," and the "best executed" of Beaumarchais' dramatic works. "The Barber" is, in fact, better composed than "The Marriage of Figaro," the two last acts of which include many lengthy passages, and are only kept up by *jeux de scène* and *jeux d'esprit*.

In this rapid transformation of "The Barber," Beaumarchais exhibited all the characteristics of the most brilliant period of his talent. His wit, has all the strength which proceeds from maturity, and he still preserves all the elasticity of youth. Ardent, versatile, and prolific, dangers and perplexities make him find unexpected resources; he can bend himself to all circumstances, and by winding himself round them, subdue them. This is the same man, who, from being a feeble playwright, became in a few days, under the influence of danger, a redoubtable and brilliant polemic; the same man, who, after having taken two years to compose at leisure a comedy, which was full of faults, made it almost a masterpiece in twenty-four hours, under the pressure of a discontented and disappointed public.

The plan of "The Barber" is not new: it is the well-known subject of the amorous old guardian, who wishes to marry his ward. Beaumarchais, who, like Molière, took his property wherever he found it, perhaps borrowed the ground-work, and a portion of the situations of his piece, from an old comedy of Fatouville's, played at the Italian Theatre in 1692, which was called "La Précaution Inutile," which is the second title of "The Barber," and which presents some analogy to the latter work. Probably also, the author of "The Barber" had read with profit Sedaine's opera comique, "On ne s'avise jamais de tout." Sedaine's Doctor Tue, a physician, a guardian, and in love with his ward Lise, belongs to the same family as Doctor Bartholo. Lise, though more completely ingenuous than Rosina is not without resemblance to Bartholo's ward. Dorval, Lise's lover, might well have contributed something towards the character of Almaviva. In order to escape the jealousy of the guardian, they both resort to stratagems of the same kind. If Almaviva disguises himself as a soldier, and afterwards as a musician, Dorval dresses himself up as an old captain from Morocco, and afterwards as an old woman; he sings and accompanies himself on the guitar, like Almaviva. In Sedaine's opera, there is even a scene in which Dorval, speaking to the duenna who watches over Lise, in order to make himself understood by the latter, uses words of a double signification, which recal the scene between Almaviva, Rosina, and Bartholo, in the third act of " The Barber." Finally, " The Barber" ends with a marriage, and the intervention of an alcalde, " *On ne s'avaise jamais de tout,*" and the intervention of a commissary. But as for amorous and jealous guardians, rebellious wards, inventive lovers, disguises, and commissaries, or alcaldes, they can be found everywhere, and are at every one's disposition; all depends upon the manner of making use of them. Beaumarchais was not wrong then, in replying to those who reproached him with having copied Sedaine's' work, by this witty sally, which is quite in his style: "An amateur," he says, "profiting by the period when there were a great many persons in the *foyer,* reproached me, in the most serious manner, with my piece resembling ' People never think of everything.'—"Resemble it, Sir? I maintain that my piece is ' People never think of everything' itself!" " And how so?" "Because people never think of my piece." The amateur stopped short, and there was the more laughter from the fact, that the person who reproached me with '" People never think of everything,' is a man who has never thought of anything."

If in effect, there is some vague similitude between Sedaine's opera and " The Barber," one thing which is not in Sedaine, and which is found nowhere before "The Barber" is the principal personage of the piece, Figaro the stage-valet, who stands out from the midst of all other stage-valets, and who is certainly Beaumarchais' exclusive property and creation. Whatever may be said of this character, he has acquired in the history of art the position of type, like Panurge, Falstaff, Don Juan, Gil Blas, and has taken rank among these imperishable characters. When he has appeared in his full development, after the "*Folle journée*," we shall have occasion to study him rather more thoroughly; but it is not only Figaro who is original in "The Barber." Bartholo, as La Harpe very justly remarks, is not a conventional guardian, like other stage-guardians. Although made a dupe, he is far from being a fool; he is very cunning on the contrary, and it requires much skill to deceive him. Hence there is a rivalry in the way of precautions and invectives between him, Rosina, Almaviva, and Figaro, which clash, fall to nothing, are renewed, and carried on with an ardour that increases from scene to scene until the *dénoûement*.

As for the dialogue of "The Barber," it is not more animated, but it seems to us of a better tone, less pretentious and more flowing than that of "The Marriage of Figaro." Beaumarchais' fault is known to be the abuse of a thing of which every one cannot make such abuse as himself, that is, the abuse of wit.

Not only does he give too much to each of his characters, but he gives each of them almost the same kind of
wit, that is to say, his own ; they are all equally fertile in unexpected sallies, in words with double meaning, in proverbs humourously distorted. The author
has not that supreme power of creation, which allows
Molière to bring to light the most diverse beings,
not only as to character, but also as to the nature of
their wit. He speaks too often through the mouth of
his characters, and sometimes a scene, linked more or
less cleverly with the general action of the piece, has
no other object than that of furnishing him with an opportunity for introducing with advantage a series of
bons mots. These sallies, which are sometimes far-
fetched, and almost dragged in by the head and
shoulders, are more frequent in " The Marriage of
Figaro" than in " The Barber," in which all progresses
and works together more satisfactorily ; however,
they are still to be found. In remarking that several
of these *bons mots* are already known, and have been
published in other works, La Harpe says, " Apparently Beaumarchais used to make a list of them
when he read." La Harpe has here guessed right.
The author of "The Barber of Seville " was in the
habit of writing without order, on separate sheets, not
only those serious or comic thoughts which struck
him in his reading, but all those which occurred to
him of themselves, and which he kept in reserve, to

use at another period. Thus the greater number of the phrases and sentences of "The Barber," or "The Marriage of Figaro," which one would at first think, had escaped from the author's *verve* in the ardour of composition, are found here and there in a sort of collection, mixed up with a multitude of historical, political, or philosophical reflections, which prove that Beaumarchais' intellect was fed upon the most different elements.

However this may be, "The Barber," which failed at the first representation, after being taken up and retouched by the author, had a complete success at the second. The audience recognised in it an original restoration of the old comedy of "Intrigue," freshened, extended, and revivified, and the hisses of the previous evening changed into applause. " I went yesterday," writes Madame du Deffant, "to see Beaumarchais' comedy, which was being represented for the second time; the first time it was hissed, yesterday it had an extravagant success. It was exalted to the clouds and applauded beyond all bounds." We must confess that Madame du Deffant adds: "Nothing could be more ridiculous; the piece is detestable. . . . . . This Beaumarchais, whose Memorials are so pleasing, is deplorable in his piece of the "Barber of Seville." Madame du Deffant's opinion was not ratified by the public. For the rest, the difficult and sated taste of Horace Walpole's witty corre-

spondent was not well calculated to appreciate a
style of comedy so frank and unfettered as that of
" The Barber," and Beaumarchais was able to console
himself for not being appreciated by her, as in the
letter, which follows the one we have just quoted, she
adds these words: "M. Gluck's 'Orpheus,' and M.
de Beaumarchais' 'Barber of Seville,' have been
very much vaunted; I was forced to see them, and
they have tired me to death." The reader sees that
it really was not easy to interest Madame du Deffant.*
The pit, which was not suffering like herself from the
disease of *ennui*, was much less difficult, and after
the second representation, "The Barber" continued
to draw crowds until the close of the winter season,
that is to say, until March 20, 1775.

The reader knows that it was formerly the custom
to close the theatres every year, and especially the
Théâtre Français, during three weeks, from Passion
week until the fête of Quasimodo. It was also a
custom at the Théâtre Français, at the last representation before the closing, for one of the actors to appear on the stage and address the public in a grand
speech, which was called the *compliment de clôture.*†

* It must also be remembered that this lady was then blind, and
that this infirmity scarcely permits a person to judge of a piece by the
representation.

† These speeches, which were addressed to the public every year,
were sometimes strange enough. Grimm quotes one, in which the
actor, Florence, said to the pit: "Gentlemen, taste is preserved

Beaumarchais, who was fond of innovation in everything, conceived the idea of replacing this discourse, which was ordinarily of a majestic nature, by a sort of prologue in one act, which was played with the costumes of "The Barber" at the final representation of 1775 and 1776. This complimentary piece in dialogue, is no longer to be found in the archives of the Comédie Française, but it has been preserved in Beaumarchais' papers, written entirely in his hand, and copied in duplicate, with a sheet containing the distribution of the parts. I cannot explain how it is that Gudin has not introduced it in his edition of his friend's works. It had doubtless escaped his researches, for it is nothing less than a little comedy in one act, the structure of which is original, while the dialogue offers all the merits of style by which "The Barber of Seville" is distinguished.

The following was the occasion on which this complimentary piece was composed. In introducing at the Théâtre Français a piece so broadly comic as "The Barber," Beaumarchais had wished to break through the somewhat narrow bounds by which this theatre was limited, which, in the name of *bon ton* and *bonne compagnie*, every piece was forbidden which re-

amongst you, as the Priestesses of Vesta preserved the sacred fire." The pit, which was not composed of vestals, laughed a great deal at the comparison. After 1789, the actors sometimes made use of the occasion to deliver political and patriotic tirades.

called more or less the ancient comedy of intrigue. The ingenious farces of Molière, such as the "Fourberies de Scapin," or "Porceaugnac," were allowed to re-appear from time to time on the stage because they were Molière's, and because after all, as these charming farces had amused Louis XIV. and his court, people did not dare to declare themselves more difficult to please than the great king; but it was not permitted for living authors to walk even at a distance in the footsteps of the master. And as the Théâtre Français alone was entitled to play comedy, properly so called, there were scarcely any intermediary shades between the gross burlesques of the boulevards and the style of comedy which flourished then; a style which was somewhat cold, stilted, and affected, without being fundamentally more moral as to ideas and situations. It has been seen with what unruly impetuosity Beaumarchais at first attempted to abolish this scrupulous distinction between the styles, in a comedy which exhibited too much exaggeration, and the faults of which justly shocked the public; and how, after making considerable alterations in it, he had secured its reception and success, although it still offered some *nuances* which were very strong. However, that was not sufficient for the author of "The Barber;" it was not sufficient for him to restore to the Théâtre Français a little of the lively gaiety of its former days; and to make the pit applaud outrageously when Dugazon sneezed in the part of the old valet La Jeunesse. He desired still more; he desired not only that the public should laugh from the bottom of their lungs, but that there should be singing on the stage of the Comedians in Ordinary of the King. This was an enormity, and in essential contradiction, it was said, to the dignity of the Comédie Française. Nevertheless, as Beaumarchais had a very obstinate will, in order to please him an attempt had been made to sing the airs he had introduced into "The Barber" at the first representation; but whether the actors acquitted themselves badly of this unaccustomed labour, or whether the public did not enjoy this innovation, all the airs had been ruthlessly hissed,* and it had been necessary to suppress them when the piece was reproduced. There was one, however, to which the author was much attached: it was Rosina's air in the third act, "Quand dans la plaine." The amiable actress who had created the part of Rosina, Mademoiselle Doligny, who was but little accustomed to sing in public, and still less accustomed to be hissed, refused positively to recommence the experiment, and Beaumarchais had been obliged to resign himself to the sacrifice of this *morceau*; but he never resigned himself to anything except temporarily. As the performance for the close

---

* Except the grotesque couplet, sung by Bartholo in the third act, which was preserved.

of the season drew near, he proposed to the actors to prepare for them the complimentary piece of which we have spoken, but on one condition, that his famous . air should be introduced and sung in the little piece which was to be played by all the actors of " The Barber." As Mademoiselle Doligny still refused to sing the *morceau* in question, and as Beaumarchais would have feared to offend her by bringing in another Rosina, he suppressed the part, and replaced it by the intervention in person of another actress, who was bolder, and sang very agreeably, Mademoiselle Luzzi.*

In order to understand this little unpublished "*proverbe,*" which was written to follow " The Barber," it must be imagined that we are at the closing representation of March 29, 1775. " The Barber " has just been acted for the thirteenth time. Just as the public are expecting, according to custom, to see one of the actors appear on the stage in his private dress, commissioned to bid them adieu, with solemn phrases, in the name of the Comédie Français, the curtain rises, and the fat Desessarts, in the cos-

---

* Mademoiselle Luzzi was, in 1775, a very pretty *soubrette*, gifted with very varied talents; for, while she played with distinction in comedy, she sang and danced if required. One day even, when there was a deficiency of tragic actresses, she played the part of Amaénaïde with Lekain, in Tancrède, acquitted herself very well, and had much success.

tume of Bartholo, comes on in an attitude of despair :—

SCENE I.

BARTHOLO (*Desessarts*), *alone, walking about with a paper in his hand. Curtain rises. He speaks to a person behind the scenes.*

Rougeau! Renard! [*] Do not raise the curtain yet, my friends, I am not ready. . . . Devil of a man to promise us a closing address, to keep us waiting till the last day, and when the time comes to leave me to do it. . . . "Gentlemen, if your indulgence did not reassure my genius in alarm. . . ." I can never utter that address. . . . "Gentlemen, your criticisms, and your applause, are equally useful to us, inasmuch as . . ." Plague take the man! "Gentlemen . . . . to make you understand all I feel, it would be necessary . . . it would be necessary . . ." Ah! to do it properly, this address ought to have some connection to the coat in which I am to deliver it; let us see: "Gentlemen, in the same way that physicians treat all kinds of patients, but do not cure all kinds of illnesses. . . ." May a good putrid fever take thee by the neck, dog of an author, treacherous author! . . . . "Treat all kinds of patients, but do not cure all kinds of illnesses. . . . So, actors with all kinds of new pieces without being sure that success. . . ." Ah! I am covered with perspiration, I can do nothing of any use. . . . . "Gentlemen . . . Gentlemen. . . ."

SCENE II.

BARTHOLO (*Desessarts*), FIGARO (*Préville*), COUNT ALMAVIVA (*Bellecour*).

FIGARO (*laughiug*).—Ah! Ah! Ah! . . Well, gentlemen!

[*] These were, doubtless, two of the scene-shifters.

BARTHOLO.—What! Have you come to annoy me again, you people?

COUNT.—We come to offer you our advice, good doctor.

BARTHOLO.—No need of such jocular preceptors. I know you now.

COUNT.—We are not joking, I swear, and it is as much our interest as yours that the address should please the public.

FIGARO.—Or that it would make it laugh at the person who utters it. In truth, we only come here with a good intention.

BARTHOLO.—Yes! . . . that is well . . . The fact is, I have a peculiarity, which is very peculiar. When I have nothing to do, my mind is as active as the devil, and as soon as I wish to begin composing . . .

FIGARO.—It takes that opportunity of remaining quiet. I know what it is, doctor. You must not be astonished at it; it is an accident which happens to many honest persons like you, who sit down to work without ideas. But, do you know what you must do? Instead of remaining in the same place while composing, which renders conception difficult, and production painful to a young person of your corpulence, you must move about, doctor, backwards and forwards; take violent exercise.

BARTHOLO.—That is what I have been doing for the last hour.

FIGARO.—And take up the pen directly you feel the animal spirits rising to your head.

BARTHOLO.—What do you mean? animal spirits. . . .

COUNT.—Be quiet, Figaro, this is a nice time for joking!

BARTHOLO.—Ungrateful barber, to whom I have shown a thousand kindnesses, you laugh at my trouble, instead of delivering me from it.

COUNT.—Where were you, doctor?

BARTHOLO.—I was just imagining for the closing, something which would at least enable me to exhibit great talent to the public.

FIGARO.—Exhibit great talent! but you need not trouble yourself, doctor; think only on the extreme pleasure you gave it, when you exhibited before its eyes your very great talent for singing, while dancing like a bear, and clapping your two thumbs together:

> Veux-tu, ma Rosinette,
> Fire emplette
> Du roi des maris?

BARTHOLO.—This fellow would hang himself rather than fail in annoying those whom he might gratify.

COUNT.—Really, Figaro, you are driving him to despair, and time is flying. Now tell me, doctor, do you know what sort of things the closing address should be composed of?

BARTHOLO.—Ah! if I could only compose it as well as I could define it.

FIGARO.—Ah! if I could only run as I can drink, I should do sixty leagues an hour.

BARTHOLO.—I know that we must invoke the indulgence of the public, speak modestly of ourselves, and say an obliging word about all the new works represented in the year.

FIGARO.—That is the most difficult part; to please the authors, we never say enough: to please the public we often say too much.

BARTHOLO.—We should find the true medium.

FIGARO.—Or not speak of them at all. In faith it would be the safest.

COUNT.—Not to speak of them at all would be hard; but it is enough to recal the works without criticising them anew. It is no longer our part to pronounce on their merits. The fact of our adopting them proves that we think well of them, and the piercing eye of the public dispenses us now from crutinising their defects. But, in regard to all successes, even the most disputed, the most doubtful, we owe the authors our just praises for an ardent desire to please the public, which we share with them.

BARTHOLO.—Morbleu! my Bachelor of Arts, why did you not say that you were going to say all that! I would have taken my pen, and my work would have been far advanced. . . . . You say then?

COUNT.—In faith, I no longer remember.

BARTHOLO.—What a pity! and you, Figaro?

FIGARO.—Well, it appeared to me very flat.

BARTHOLO. — I should think so, directly there are no puns.

FIGARO.—It is true, I can't do anything else.

BARTHOLO.—Try, at least, to make yourself useful for once, by telling us what pieces have been given this year.

FIGARO.—We gave, we gave. . . .

Here Figaro, Bartholo, and the Count, go through a review of the pieces given in 1775, with criticisms by Figaro, exhibiting a diplomatic sort of reserve, which is rather droll.

BARTHOLO.—That, however, makes seven novelties in ten months; and it is said that we are idle.

FIGARO.—We would dispose of plenty more, if we could unite interests which are irreconcileable; but while the writer who has the next turn repeats incessantly: "On with the play; end it once for all; it is my turn to begin,"—the author who is on the stage cries out on his side: "Gently with the play! gently! let me live a little longer." All this is very difficult.

SCENE III.

The preceding actors, MDLLE. LUZZI.

MDDLE. LUZZI.—Well, gentlemen! has not the address been spoken?

FIGARO.—Worse than that, it is not written.

MDLLE. LUZZI.—The address?

BARTHOLO.—A cursed author had promised me one; at the very moment for delivering it he tells us to get it elsewhere.

MDLLE. LUZZI.—I am in the secret: he is annoyed at our having cut out the air of the *Spring* from his piece.

BARTHOLO.—What air of the *Spring?* What piece? You fancy you know everything.

MDLLE. LUZZI.—Rosina's arietta, in "The Barber of Seville."

BARTHOLO.—It is quite right, Mademoiselle; the public does not like singing at the Comédie Française.

MDLLE. LUZZI.—Yes, doctor, in tragedies; but how long is it since it has wished to deprive a gay subject of what is calculated to increase its liveliness? Come, gentlemen, Mr. Public likes everything that amuses him.

BARTHOLO.—Besides, is it our fault if Rosina's courage failed her?

MDLLE. LUZZI (*with an affected smile*).—Is the song pretty?

COUNT.—Will you try it?

BARTHOLO.—Would you not like to hear it sung? How am I ever to finish my address?

COUNT.—Go on all the same, doctor.

FIGARO (*to* MDLLE. LUZZI, *on one side*, sotto voce).

MDLLE. LUZZI.—But I am like Rosina myself. I shall be all in a tremble.

FIGARO.—Fie! tremble? a bad plan, Mademoiselle.

MDLLE. LUZZI.—Well! you do not finish your little pun; the fear of evil, and the evil of fear?*

FIGARO.—Oh! you call that a pun?

MDLLE. LUZZI.—It is true that I who† am afraid of my

* An allusion to a *jeu de mot* in "The Barber of Seville." "Quand on cède à la peur du mal, on ressent déjà le mal de la peur."

† Mademoiselle Luzzi's speech cannot be rendered into English

evil singing, already feel very strongly the evil produced by
such a fear.

FIGARO (*laughing*).—I believe you; but you will not sing
the less for that. You are so kind, Luzzi, that in all matters
you never offer any difficulties, except of an engaging nature.

MDLLE. LUZZI.—It would only depend upon me to take
that for an insult.

COUNT.—Rosina, who is scarcely acquainted with her talent,
is very timid: but you who sing frequently, confess, you
rogue, that you are now only behaving with the hypocrisy of
timidity. (MDLLE. LUZZI *sings a lively prelude*.)

FIGARO.—This Luzzi will always be the same; singing, acting, always young, always beautiful: on my honour, she is
the diamond of society.

BARTHOLO.—Cursed chatterer!

MDLLE. LUZZI (*laughing*).—Ah! ah! ah! Let him get out
of that, doctor, and explain to us how I am a diamond.

FIGARO (*gaily*).—Like all pretty women. Nature amuses
herself by fertilising the abundant mine, in which these
diamonds are taken. Youth is the lapidary which developes
and cuts them; elegant dress is the socket in which they are
placed; our imagination is the leaf which polishes them;
finally, beautiful Luzzi, is not love . . . the jeweller who
sets them?

MDLLE. LUZZI.—Hem! malicious jester! and you forget
marriage?

FIGARO.—It is, if you like, the dealer who introduces them
into commerce.

BARTHOLO.—Devil take the setter, the dealer, and the
diamond; I have lost the most sublime idea!

without a sacrifice either of sound or of sense. As, in endeavouring to
preserve both, we have sacrificed a great deal of each, we now subjoin
the speech in the original French:—"Il est vrai que moi qui ai peur
de mal chanter, je ressens déjà beaucoup le mal que me fait cette
frayeur-là."—TRANS.

COUNT (*to* MDDLE. LUZZI).—I hope his anger will not deprive us of the pleasure of hearing you.

MDLLE. LUZZI.—At least, gentlemen, it is you who wish me to sing.

BARTHOLO.—Oh! not at all.

FIGARO.—Certainly.

COUNT.—We shall see whether the air would have been pleasing.

MDLLE. LUZZI (*sings*)—

> " Quand dans la plaine
> Ramène, &c." *

COUNT.—Very pretty, on my honour.

FIGARO.—It is a charming *morceau.*

BARTHOLO.—Oh! go to the devil with your charming *morceau.* I do not know what I am doing; thus, I have been interlarding my address with lambs, dogs, and pipes. . . . Don Basil at this time . . .

The scene with Basil is only a variation of the mystification seen in " The Barber." Basil is supposed to be unaware that it is the closing performance, and wishes to announce to the public the piece for the following night. Figaro mystifies him as much as possible, and every one repeats to him the celebrated phrase : *allez vous coucher.*† After Basil

* We must naturally suppose that Mademoiselle Luzzi was very much applauded by the public.

† This " allez vous coucher," of the mystification scene of " The Barber," had had so much success that its fame had reached Voltaire, and rather alarmed him. This was the reason : The father of Irène, in the tragedy of that name, which he was then composing, was in the first instance named Basil. Voltaire wrote on this subject as follows

has retired, Bartholo continues in his agitated state, but the address does not make much progress. He at length appeals to Figaro and the Count.

BARTHOLO.—Finally, since you are there, if you were only in my place, both of you, what should you say?

FIGARO.—If we were in your place, doctor, it is evident we should not know what to say.

BARTHOLO.—No, no! If you were I, that is to say, had to make the address——

COUNT.—I should collect my thoughts for a moment, and I think I should say something of this kind: "Is it necessary for me to say much about our anxiety to please when I am speaking in the name of the whole company? For does not our theatrical existence belong to each of you, although to derive enjoyment from it, each one deprives himself of only the smallest portion of the superfluous sums which he devotes to his amusements? To be convinced then, gentlemen, that a more noble motive than self-interest makes us wish to give you constant pleasure, consider, that in our eyes there is no proportion between the trifling advantage of the profit produced by any one place, and the extreme pleasure which is derived from the slightest applause of the person who fills it. For this reward, which is so precious to us, we support

---

to M. d'Argental :—" M. de Villette states that the name of Basil has become a very dangerous one, since the Basil of 'The Barber of Seville.' He says that the pit cries out sometimes, 'Basil, go to bed,' and that, with the noisy portion, a joke of that kind is quite sufficient to cause the failure of the best piece in the world.' I think M. de Villette is right; it will only be necessary to make the copyist of the theatre put Léonce in place of Basil. Luckily the name of Basil never occurs at the end of a line, and Léonce can be substituted for it everywhere. That, I think, is the only inconvenience this piece is likely to occasion.

the disgust of study, the over-taxing of the memory, the uncertainty of success, the wearisomeness of repeating the same
thing, and all the fatigues of the most laborious calling. Our
only business is to give you pleasure; always in ecstacy
when we succeed, our disposition never changes towards you,
although yours sometimes changes towards us. And when,
in spite of his endeavours, some one of us has the misfortune
to displease you, see with what modest silence he devours his
chagrin at your reproaches, and you will not attribute this to
a want of sensibility on our part, whose only study is to
excite yours. In all other quarrels the aggressor remains in
restless expectation of the resentment he provokes; here the
person attacked lowers his eyes with respectful timidity, and
the only weapon with which he meets the most severe treatment
is a fresh effort to please you, and regain your good opinions.
Ah! gentlemen, for our glory, and for your pleasure, believe
that we are all desirous of being perfect actors; but we are
forced to confess that the only thing we would rather never
invoke is unfortunately the one, of which we oftenest have
need, your indulgence " (*he bows*).

BARTHOLO.—Good, good, good, excellent.

FIGARO.—For shame! take care you do not write down,
doctor, all that he has been saying.

BARTHOLO.—And why?

FIGARO.—It is not worth a jot.

MDLLE. LUZZI.—What! this speech? It appeared to me
so good.

BARTHOLO.—I wager, for my part, that it would be very
much applauded.

FIGARO.—Because it has a certain ring on the ear, and
sounds like a compliment. . . . Not a thought which is
not false.

BARTHOLO.—Author's jealousy.

COUNT.—Ah! let us see.

FIGARO.—You prefer the applause of the public, to the
profit derived from the places it occupies?

COUNT.—Certainly.

FIGARO.—Very well; but if each one abstained from bringing here the value of his place, where would you look for the pleasure of his applause? Let the absurdity, however, pass; but to think of lowering in our eyes the sweet, the useful receipts, and play the contemptuous with regard to a thing so deservedly profitable! Examine all conditions, from the grave ambassador with his cypher, to the comic author with his scribble, from the ingenious minister who invents a new tax, to the obscure purloiner, who also dives into the pockets: where is anything done which is not for the profit of the well-beloved receipts? And the general, covered with glory, who asks for a governorship, and the heir of an illustrious name for a rich wife, and the pious abbé, who runs after a living, and the grave magistrate, who grows pale over speculations, and the assiduous legatee, who intrigues about his great uncle, and the virtuous mother, who delivers up her daughter to the nuptial inutility of an amorous old gentleman, and he who navigates, and he who preaches, and he who dances, in fine, all even to myself, of whom I say nothing, but who do not forget myself more than another—is there a single man in the world who does not act in order to augment the good, the sweet, the thrice, four times, six times, ten times, agreeable receipts? With your insipid compliments you solicit the public as an austere judge; as for me, I love her as my good mother and nurse. She sometimes boxed my ears, but her caresses were sweet, and her milk inexhaustible. Logomachy, battology, jingling of words, are all these fine speeches! And then, what is the meaning of the injured person who lowers his eyes timidly, when the public is out of humour? When the public raises its voice against an actor, is not the latter the aggressor? The public comes in search of pleasure, and it deserves to have it; it has paid for it in advance. Whose is the fault if it is not given to it? Your compliments are all balderdash! What nonsense can be passed off on the world, if the phrases be well turned! Finally, you will do as you like; but for my part, I would not employ all these long phrases of respect and devotion, which are overdone every day, and which lead no one away; I should only say, "Gentlemen, you all come here to pay for the pleasure of hearing a good work, and in truth, it is very good of you; when the author keeps his word, and the actor exhausts himself, you applaud into the bargain: very generous on your part, assuredly. When the curtain has fallen, you take away the pleasure, we the praise and the money; each one goes off gaily to supper: all are satisfied. A delightful barter in truth! Accordingly, I have only one word to say: our interest is your guarantee for our zeal; weigh it in this balance, gentlemen, and you will see if there can ever be any doubt about it." Well, doctor, what do you think of my little pun?

BARTHOLO.—That rascal manages so well, that he always contrives to be in the right.

AN ACTOR OF THE AFTER-PIECE.—Have you sworn, then, to make us sleep here with your address, which you are still doing, and will never do? The public is getting impatient.

BARTHOLO.—Well! one moment. It is for the public we are working.

ACTOR.—But, go and work in a box, in the lobby, wherever you please; during the time we will begin the after-piece.

BARTHOLO.—What a man! Leave us alone.

ACTOR.—You won't go away? Strike up, strike up, as loudly as you can, gentlemen of the orchestra; when they see no one is listening to them, I can swear that not one of them will be tempted to remain chattering on the stage.

FIGARO.—He has really, in one word, unveiled the whole mystery of the drama.

(*The orchestra begins playing; they all leave the stage, and the curtain falls.*)

This *bluette,* in connexion with "The Barber of Seville," which had remained unknown until now, appeared to us worthy of being published, or, at least, a great part of it.*   The plan is ingenious, and some skill was required for preserving the character which each of the personages of "The Barber" had in the piece, while they were at the same time made to speak as actors.   It has been seen how Beaumarchais solved the difficulty.   He was about to find himself before long in a greater difficulty—that of bringing to reason the very actors for whom he wrote closing addresses.   His destiny ordained that he should only get out of one law-suit to fall into another, and that everything in his life, even to "The Barber of Seville," the gayest of *imbroglios,* should become the subject of an action.

* We might have given it entire, and placed it in the Appendix, but a great many readers would not perhaps have taken the trouble to look for it there. We preferred abridging it a little, and intercalating it in the body of the book.

APPENDIX.

No. 1 (page 40).

Cherbourg, September 12, 1781.

I have long, my dear Beaumarchais, proposed to myself a step, which I have only accomplished to-day : it is that of repairing the indiscretion of the remarks I made eight years since on the subject of your affair with the Duke de Chaulnes. My heart reproaches me with it the more, from the fact that, besides my judgment having been hasty, and consequently unjust, with regard to your conduct in this strange affair, you had until then been my friend, and you were at that moment deprived of your liberty, while you were attacked in your property and honour. During my stay in the Bastille, which followed by some months the inconsiderate judgments I pronounced against you, I read the excellent Memorials you produced in your affair with Goëzman ; they inflamed my heart and amused my mind ; your gaiety, your sensibility, all your affections took possession of me turn by turn ; from that period I reproached myself with having injured your feelings by judging you incorrectly. Do not look, my dear Beaumarchais, for the cause of my step, either in politics or in any personal interest. Separated from you and from Paris for a long time, nothing would induce me to take it unless my heart told me to do so. As, however, a pretext was necessary for writing to you, I beg you to tell me when and where I may subscribe for the edition of Voltaire's works which you have brought out. This work will be valuable, coming from your hands. Send me word, forget the past, and rely on the esteem and friendship of your servant,

DUMOURIEZ,

Colonel of Dragoons, Commandant of Cherbourg.

No. 2 (page 53).

The Duke de la Vrillière to M. de Sartines. March 22, 1773, at Versailles.

M. de Beaumarchais, Monsieur, having represented to me that his action was on the point of being decided, and that it was of the greatest importance for him to be able to communicate personally with his judges, you can give him permission to leave For-l'Evêque, solely with this object, and on this condition that he goes back regularly to take his meals and sleep there; and in order to make sure that he conforms to this arrangement, you will be kind enough to give him a trustworthy person to accompany him in the visits he will be obliged to make.

It is impossible to be more perfectly than I am, Sir, your very humble and very obedient servant,

THE DUKE DE LA VRILLIERE.

No. 3 (page 145).

NOEL

ON BEAUMARCHAIS' ACTION AGAINST GOEZMAN.

AIR—*Des Bourgeois de Chartres.*

D'une vierge féconde
L'enfantement, dit-on,
Attira bien du monde
A Jésus, à l'ânon.
—Nous étouffons ici, dit l'enfant à sa mère;

Renvoyez-moi ce parlement.
—Non, dit Maupeou tout doucement,
A l'âne il pourra plaire.

— Oh ! dit l'âne, j'en doute,
Je renonce aux procès ;
Voulez-vous qu'il m'en coûte
Autant qu'à Beaumarchais ?
Pour moi je ne prétends faire aucun sacrifice.
— Mais, dit La Blache, il le faut bien ;
Croyez-vous qu'l n'en coûte rien
Pour gagner la justice ?

— Nous avons peu de gages,
Répond l'auguste corps,
Et pour nos équipages
Il en faut de très-forts.
Nous pouvons exiger ces petits sacrifices ;
Au plus offrant nous accordons
Ce qu'à d'autres nous refusons :
Cela tient lieu d'épices.

— O ciel ! quelle impudence !
Dit Goëzman l'imposteur ;
J'en demande vengeance,
Je suis le rapporteur.
Parbleu ! je ne prends rien, ma femme peut le dire.
A ces mots, le bœuf et l'ânon
Lurent l'interrogation
En éclatant de rire.

La dame, un peu féroce,
D'abord avec esprit
Répond que c'est atroce
A tout ce que l'on dit ;

Mais bientôt, se coupant dans sa vive réplique,
        Dit, à sa confrontation,
        Que la perte de sa raison
            Vient d'un état critique.

        Lejay contre la porte
        Restait comme un nigaud :
        — Qu'est-ce donc qu'il apporte ?
        Dit le bœuf un peu haut.
Goëzman lors répondit :—C'est un point qu'on discute
        Pour ma justification ;
        C'est une déclaration
            Dont j'ai fait la minute.

        Avec son humeur noire
        Baculard approcha
        Présentant un mémoire
        Que l'âne fort glosa :
—Adieu, mes compagnons, j'ai peur de la gourmade,
        J'aime mieux ne jamais parler
        Que d'être le sot conseiller
            D'une telle ambassade.*

        D'un grand air d'importance
        Certain homme arriva,
        Disant : — Ma bienfaisance
        Jusqu'à vous s'étendra.
— Quesaco ? dit Jésus, quel est ce gentilhomme
        On répond :—C'est un roturier,
        Fripier d'écrits, vil usurier,
            Une bête de somme.

* D'Arnaud-Baculard assumed in his Memorial the title of Ambassador of the Court of Saxony.

— J'apporte ma gazette,
Dit Marin hautement.
— Ah ! bon Dieu ! qu'elle est bête !
Dit Joseph en bâillant.
Non, jamais je n'ai vu platitude pareille ;
Qu'il retourne à La Ciotat,
Sur l'orgue avec l'âne il pourra
Concerter à merveille.

— Pour le coup, j'en appelle,
Cria le Grand-Cousin ;*
En haut de mon libelle
Je vous parle latin.
— Sors, s'écria Jésus, au diable ta personne !
Laridon et le Sacristain
Ont un goût si fort de Marin
Que l'odeur m'empoisonne.

Pour assoupir l'affaire,
Don Goëzman, poliment,
Vient offrir à la mère
De tenir son enfant.
—Serait-ce sur les fonts ? ciel ! quelle audace extrême !
Fi ! Monsieur, vous changez de nom ;
J'aimerais mieux que le poupon
Se passât de baptême†

Le président suprême,‡
Avec ses yeux de bœuf
Et son esprit de même,
Porte un édit tout neuf.

* Bertrand d'Airolles.

† An allusion to the false signature appended to a certificate of baptism by the Councillor Goëzman.

‡ Berthier de Sauvigny, chief president of the Maupeou Parliament.

—Donnez-le, dit l'ânon, j'en veux un exemplaire ;
    Il suffit qu'il n'ait pas de sens,
    Je le lirai de temps en temps
      Pour m'exciter à braire.

      Le Sauveur dans la presse
      Beaumarchais reconnut.
      — Cet homme m'intéresse,
      Dit-il, dès qu'il parut.
En vain Châteaugiron contre lui se rebecque ;*
      Qu'il prenne place près de moi ;
      Ses Mémoires seront, ma foi,
      Dans ma bibliothèque.

      Certain ex-militaire †
      Dont on sait la valeur,
      De Goëzman le faussaire
      Digne solliciteur,
Voyant près du Sauveur Beaumarchais à sa place,
      Dit en jurant comme un païen :
      —Gens du guet, prenez ce coquin ;
      Il me fait la grimace.

      Jésus s'écrie :—Arrête !
      Modère ton ardeur,
      Capitaine Tempête,
      Surtout, de la douceur ;
Pour tes concitoyens sois aussi débonnaire,
      Aussi doux sur les fleurs de lis
      Qu'on te vit pour les ennemis
      Quand tu fus militaire.

---

  * One of the Councillors of the Maupeou Parliament who was most hostile to Beaumarchais.

  † The President de Nicolaï, a declared enemy of Beaumarchais, and a former colonel of cavalry.

Joseph avec colère
Dit à tous de sortir,
Et qu'après cette affaire
L'enfant voulait dormir.
— Ah ! c'est donc sur ce ton qu'on nous met à la porte !
Quoi ! Beaumarchais seul restera !
Mais son mémoire on brûlera.
L'auteur dit :—Peu m'importe.

O troupe incorruptible,
Retournez à Paris ;
Ce coup sera sensible
A tous les bons esprits.
La bêtise chez vous a passé la mesure.
Peut-être que cet accident
Nous rendra l'ancien parlement ;
On dit la chose sûre.

No. 4 (page 207).

I, the undersigned, acknowledge that M. de Beaumarchais
has remitted to me for the king, all the papers contained in
the two inventories hereto annexed, and which relate to the
transaction of the 5th of last October, passed between M. de
Beaumarchais and Mademoiselle d'Eon de Beaumont ; of
which inventories I will have him provided with duplicates to
serve for his discharge, declaring that the king has been
much satisfied with the zeal he showed on this occasion, and
the intelligence and dexterity with which he acquitted himself of the commission his Majesty had entrusted to him ; of
which he has ordered me to deliver the present attestation,
to serve him at all times, and wherever it may be necessary
to him.

Done at Versailles, December 18, 1775.

(Signed)   GRAVIER DE VERGENNES.

No. 5 (page 217).

Unpublished Letter from Beaumarchais to the Chevalier d'Eon, whom he takes for a Woman.

"Paris August 18, 1776.

I should have wished, my dear (*ma chère*) d'Eon, to have never had any but agreeable things to write to you. At this moment even, forgetting all that is unjust and outrageous in your conduct towards me, I should like M. de Comte de Vergennes to have chosen to reply to you, some one whose offices would have been less odious to you; I should wish above all, to have gained from this minister the points to which you appear so much attached; but, independently of the weight which his character gives to his reasons, they appear to me in themselves incontestable, and without reply.

"Can the king of France," said this minister to me, "grant to a girl a safe conduct, which refers to the profession of an officer?" Who, then, served the king? Is it Mademoiselle or Monsieur d'Eon? If his Majesty, on hearing after the act, the fault his parents have committed in his person against decency, morals, and respect for the laws, consents to forget it, and not to hold him guilty for having continued it when conscious of its nature; must the indulgence of the king towards her, go so far as to charge the late king with the absurdity of her indecent disguise, by making use of this phrase, of the model which she has the assurance to send us herself? Order . . . . 'never to quit the dress of her sex again, as was formerly required by the service of the king, my predecessor,' &c. &c. Never, Sir, did the service of the king require that a woman should usurp the name of a man, and the coat of an officer, or the position of envoy. By thus increasing her rash claims, this woman has managed to fatigue the king's patience, my own, and the good will of all her supporters. Let her remain in England, or go elsewhere; you well know that we do not take the slightest interest in that. As to her extreme desire to come back to France, I have informed her, through you, that the king's intention was, that she should not come back there except in the dress of her sex, and that she should lead that silent, modest, and reserved life, which she ought never to have abandoned. I shall not add a word to that."

For my part, my dear, I have well reflected on it. On my honour, I cannot conceive of what use the new attempt you are making on his complaisance can be.

If you do not care about returning to France, why do you not live quietly where you are, with what the king has given to you, instead of referring incessantly to things which have passed, and renewing perpetually requests that cannot be granted?

If your intention is really to return, what is the meaning of all this punctiliousness?

Do you hope for a more fitting time, a more magnanimous king, a more equitable minister, a more anxious mediator, better conditions? Life passes, and you languish in exile.

My dear friend, I tell you this with regret; I have laboured much, I have tried many things, and I have no hope of obtaining anything more for you. I have tried in many ways, as an act of justice, the bounds of which are thought to have been long since passed. As for favours, you must feel like myself, that a line of conduct entirely opposed to your own can alone deserve them.

Believe a man who, in spite of your frightful wrongs towards him, has served you, serves you, and will serve you with all his heart, if you yourself do not interpose eternal obstacles. Your decided, and even trenchant tone, prejudices the minister against you. "You appear to him," he says, "not as a modest and unfortunate woman, who is asking services, but as a potentate who is treating with his equal about the interests of the world. If your desire to be of advantage to him, Sir, makes you forget how ridiculous and out of place this is, I must remember it myself." Those are his words.

Think well of it, my dear d'Eon; without assuming any other character than that of a man who wishes well to you, I hasten to warn you beforehand, if you want my friendship not to be absolutely useless to you, soften your tone, and, above all, come to some reasonable resolution.

Your brother-in-law can certify to you that this caution is the most important I can give you. I intend to make a tour to London during the vacations of the Parliament of Paris. I shall see you there with the greatest pleasure, and shall esteem myself very happy if I can still contribute to your future happiness.

Good bye, my dear.

(Signed)   BEAUMARCHAIS.

END OF VOL. II.

LONDON:
WILLIAM STEVENS, PRINTER, 37, BELL YARD,
TEMPLE BAR.

Lightning Source UK Ltd.
Milton Keynes UK
UKHW011158051118
331792UK00006B/1080/P